Social Skills Games & Activities
for Kids With Autism

Social Skills Games & Activities for Kids With Autism

Wendy Ashcroft, Ed.D., Angela M. Delloso,
and Anne Marie K. Quinn

PRUFROCK PRESS INC.
WACO, TEXAS

HALF HOLLOW HILLS
COMMUNITY LIBRARY
55 Vanderbilt Parkway
Dix Hills, NY 11746

Library of Congress Cataloging-in-Publication Data

Ashcroft, Wendy, 1953-
  Social skills games and activities for kids with autism / by Wendy Ashcroft, Ed.D.,
Angela M. Delloso, and Anne Marie K. Quinn.
      p. cm.
  Includes bibliographical references.
  ISBN 978-1-61821-028-9 (pbk.)
  1. Autistic children--Education. 2. Social skills in children. I. Delloso, Angela M.,
1974- II. Quinn, Anne Marie K., 1966- III. Title.
  LC4717.5.A84 2013
  371.94--dc23
                              2012042342

Copyright © 2013, Prufrock Press Inc.

Edited by Lacy Compton

Layout design by Raquel Trevino

ISBN-13: 978-1-61821-028-9

No part of this book may be reproduced, translated, stored in a retrieval system, or transmitted, in any form or by any means, electronic, mechanical, photocopying, microfilming, recording, or otherwise, without written permission from the publisher.

Printed in the United States of America.

At the time of this book's publication, all facts and figures cited are the most current available. All telephone numbers, addresses, and website URLs are accurate and active. All publications, organizations, websites, and other resources exist as described in the book, and all have been verified. The authors and Prufrock Press Inc. make no warranty or guarantee concerning the information and materials given out by organizations or content found at websites, and we are not responsible for any changes that occur after this book's publication. If you find an error, please contact Prufrock Press Inc.

Prufrock Press Inc.
P.O. Box 8813
Waco, TX 76714-8813
Phone: (800) 998-2208
Fax: (800) 240-0333
http://www.prufrock.com

TABLE OF CONTENTS

CHAPTER 1

Social Skills and Children With ASD

Social Skills

Social interactions fill our lives. A typical day with others can start with greetings and exchanges at breakfast, conversing about the previous day, cooperating and collaborating on projects at school, participating in afterschool recreation activities, relating events of the day during dinner, and associating with family members in the evening.

Elliott, Racine, and Busse (1995) have defined the skills needed for such interactions as learned responses that enable people to interact in ways that result in positive, and avoid negative, responses from others. Most people learn these skills during their development. Immediately after birth, typically developing children perceive and analyze the responses of people to their actions. They observe how their mothers respond with attention to their cries, and they soon learn to communicate their needs for food and care. Before they are even 2 years old, even if their speech isn't intelligible, they look at others and imitate social exchanges. Soon, they learn to make requests and comments, wait, take turns, and share. Most of these skills are learned in the context of their natural environment by watching others, imitating and experimenting, and responding to the feedback they receive from others.

However, social interactions are complex, and it takes practice and work to maintain positive social relationships. In the early stages of social development, young children may struggle with learning social behavior. For example, children may be confused about when it is acceptable to interrupt conversations or make requests. They might walk between people who are conversing or ask for things when someone is busy with an important task. Or they may ask questions that are appropriate to ask at home to strangers and make statements that others consider to be offensive.

Even as adults, we can misinterpret the intentions, communications, and actions of other people. We might misread raised eyebrows as surprise when the person is really taking offense. Or we might see a stare as a need for further explanation rather than a communication of boredom. There are also times that we are perplexed by the reactions of other people to our communications. For example, we sometimes compliment a person who then cries, or scold a child who then laughs, or joke with a person who then becomes angry.

When the reactions of others make sense to us, we have usually gained some knowledge of the previous history or current state of another person. The history or state influences their responses, so it might be that the complimented person is exhausted and relieved or that the scolded child who laughs is anxious and is relieving the anxiety by laughing. A person who has been bullied or abused may take a joke seriously and become angered by its insensitivity.

Under the best of circumstances, it can be difficult to maintain and enjoy relationships with others. As we'll discuss in the next chapter, children with autism spectrum disorders have characteristics that make it especially challenging to develop the special friendships that make childhood so rich and wonderful.

Children With Autism Spectrum Disorders

Autism spectrum disorders (ASD) are complex conditions defined by specific behavior patterns and characteristics. Children with ASD have impairments in communication and social interaction. In addition, they have restrictive, repetitive, and stereotypic patterns of behavior as well as narrow interests and activities. Because these disorders are defined by certain sets of behaviors, it is known as a "spectrum disorder," one that affects individuals differently and to various degrees. ASD includes children with widely varying differences in these attributes, and we find each child with an ASD to be a unique, fascinating, and wonderful individual.

Autism is considered to be of neurological origin, and brain scans show structural differences between the brains of children with ASD and children who are developing typically. No single cause has been identified and it is likely that the origin of ASD will eventually be linked to combinations of genetic and environmental factors. There is evidence that autism runs in some families, thus giving strength to the supposition that there is some genetic predisposition to ASD. However, so far, researchers have not been able to determine that genetic factors alone cause autism. A number of environmental stresses have been identified. These include exposure to environmental toxins or chemicals, viral infections, metabolic imbalances, advanced parental age, maternal illness during pregnancy, and certain difficulties during birth. These factors, by themselves, do not cause ASD, but, in combination with genetic risk factors, they seem to increase risk.

In the past decade, there has been tremendous growth in the number of children diagnosed with ASD. In fact, one study reported a 1,148% increase between 1987 and 2007 (Cavagnaro, 2007). Although there are still some who believe this growth is due to increased awareness and broad diagnoses, most careful research shows that there is a true increase. The prevalence is now estimated at 1 in 88 (Centers for Disease Control and Prevention, 2012).

ASD is generally diagnosed before the age of 3 and usually affects a person throughout life. Some people with ASD are able to live independent lives but others may have needs requiring a lifetime of support. There is no simple medical test that can be used to diagnose ASD. However, using the guidelines in the text revision of the fourth edition of the American Psychiatric Association's *Diagnostic and Statistical Manual* (DSM-IV-TR, 2000), a physician can make a medical diagnosis based on an assessment of symptoms, diagnostic tests, developmental history, and input from people who know the child.

To determine if a child with ASD is eligible for services under the Individuals with Disabilities Education Improvement Act (IDEA, 2004), a multidisciplinary evaluation team comprised of various school professionals must determine that the disorder interferes with the child's ability to succeed in the general education setting and curriculum. Although states vary in the actual requirements, most multidisciplinary teams need evaluation results from the physician, a speech-language pathologist, and an educational or psychological diagnostician (IDEA, 2004).

In this book, we have provided suggestions for teaching children who have the following three kinds of ASD: classic autism, Asperger's syndrome, and Pervasive Developmental Disorder–Not Otherwise Specified. Classic autism (also referred to as autistic disorder) includes children who have significant language delays, social and communication challenges, unusual behaviors and interests, and sometimes an accompanying intellectual disability. Asperger's syndrome (AS) is a form of autism also characterized by social challenges and unusual behaviors and interests. Most children with AS do not have language delays or intellectual disabilities, but still can have difficulties with social communication. The third group is composed of children who have diagnoses of Pervasive Developmental Disorder–Not Otherwise Specified (PDD–NOS). Generally, these children have fewer and milder difficulties with social, communication, and behavior challenges.

We designed this book for teachers and parents who have children who range from about 5–12 years old. However, it may be useful for some younger children who have good language skills and some older children with language delays. We believe the games and activities can be adjusted to meet the interests of the particular children you teach.

For simplicity, we will use the term *teacher* throughout. But parents who are able to gather friends and playmates for their children will easily be able to follow the guidelines and implement the games and activities at home.

The Characteristics of Autism Make Social Interactions Challenging

Several of the characteristics of individuals with ASD described by Ashcroft, Argiro, and Keohane (2010) are helpful in understanding more about children with ASD and why children on the spectrum have difficulty with social interactions. Considering these characteristics helps us understand some of the challenges children with ASD have in learning the social skills needed to interact effectively and comfortably with others.

CHARACTERISTIC
Individuals With ASD Often Have Difficulty Communicating With Others, Both in Conveying Information and in Understanding What Others Say

The exchange of information is important to social interaction and many children with ASD have trouble with both sides of the exchange. They may have delayed (or even absent) verbal language, interfering with their ability to convey information. In addition, they often have difficulty understanding what others say to them. This is especially true of abstract concepts, but may even include limited ability in following simple directions.

Interacting with others is more effective when children use words to explain what they want to do. Obviously, it is more acceptable to use words to make polite requests than it is to scream and point. Relating to others is also enhanced when children have the vocabulary needed to make comments, express feelings, give information or directions, and to show interest in or care for others.

Understanding language is also critical to interacting with others and to the development of appropriate social skills. Early on, being able to follow directions allows children to learn to follow social conventions (sitting when it's appropriate to sit, waiting for desired things and attention, speaking with an appropriate volume, or even staying quiet in a place such as a library or classroom). In addition, if children understand language, it can be used to explain social expectations such as taking turns in conversations, not standing close to another person in an elevator, and not talking to strangers.

Consider this example of the power of language to help teach social skills. Alyse arrived in the parking lot of the community swimming pool with her two young children. Before they got out of the car, Alyse explained that they would need to hold her hand while walking into the building, wait while she signed in, put their clothes in the locker, and stand still while she put on sunscreen. All this, Alyse said, needed to be done before they got into the pool. Before unlocking the car doors, Alyse reviewed this twice and asked her children to list the steps themselves. As they followed this process, she labeled the steps and praised the children for following her directions. Their ability to understand the language and her ability to explain things clearly contributed to a highly successful transition from the car to the pool, resulting in an excellent demonstration of socially acceptable behavior.

In a contrary example, with children unable to understand her language, Alyse might be racing after the children to grab their hands for the walk into the building. She would be struggling to keep them in place while she signed in and to hold them still while putting on sunscreen. In most cases, impatient children demonstrate socially annoying behaviors such as whining, crying, wiggling, or even bolting away. The children, with practice, may eventually learn the routine; however, the ability to speak and understand language contributes greatly to socially appropriate behavior.

Many children with ASD have difficulty processing information when it is presented verbally. This is sometimes because they have difficulty distinguishing what is being said from background noise or distractions. Other times, children hear the words but can't remember them long enough to act on the information they heard. This can be immediate such as when they can't remember the first step of a two- or three-step set of directions. It can also be delayed such as when they can repeat it back, but can't remember it when they later try to carry out the directions. Sometimes, children cannot distinguish sounds or words that sound the same. For example, rhyming words or phrases (like "take it" and "make it") or sounds that are similar (like "ch" and "sh") may sound the same. In addition, some children do not attend long enough or carefully enough to hear all of the words and to retain the information so it can be used.

Consider the case of Riley who, at school, goes to recess daily. On most days, Riley plays with the small stones on the surface of the playground. He makes piles, digs holes, and scoops up stones to let them fall through his fingers to the ground. On many occasions, he would throw stones into the air, letting them rain down on himself and others. His teachers frequently tell him "no playing with rocks" and to "stop throwing those stones, you'll hurt someone." They often follow these verbal commands with explanations about hurting people and playing with others the right way. Not only did Riley probably not hear the negation in those sentences, but he also most likely did not attend long enough to understand the explanations. The knowledge that he might be hearing only the portion "playing with rocks" and "throwing those stones" helps us understand why the behavior would continue.

CHARACTERISTIC
Individuals With ASD Often Struggle to Understand the Perspective of Others, May Have an Impaired Ability to Read and Interpret the Emotions of Others, and Might Have Difficulty Understanding Social Cues

Children with ASD often have difficulty with social reciprocity (the back and forth of social interactions). Sometimes, they do not notice the reactions of others, thus allowing them to continue on in spite of those reactions. For example, in some cases, they may persist in talking about a subject of their own interest, even if the person is backing away or looking bored. In other cases, they may not show any interest in what others talk about, making the interaction equally unsatisfactory. Other times, they may notice some reaction and misinterpret it, once again continuing on without adjusting to the response of their social partner.

In addition, some children with ASD don't find social interaction pleasant or rewarding. They may not understand any value in smiles, nods, or even high fives. To complicate things, they may find those behaviors puzzling or even aversive.

Many children with ASD have difficulty understanding emotions. They may have difficulty labeling their own emotions to explain how they are feeling. In addition, they may not notice behaviors of others that might give clues to how those others are feeling. For example, while many typically developing children see the relationship between another person's tears and the word "sad," some children with ASD don't make that connection.

Children with ASD may not understand the perspective of others. For example, they might believe that if they know something, everyone should know it—or, if they can see it, everyone can see it. They may say something that sounds rude and insensitive and not understand why someone would take offense.

Children with ASD are often so focused on their own interests, needs, and wants that they don't notice or understand the desires of others. Consider Camden's situation as he played with Emily at school. At first, Emily sought out Camden in center time play activities, and Camden responded consistently to her guidance. For example, while playing in the housekeeping center, Emily told Camden to fix her lunch. Over the next few days, she directed him in building with blocks and playing with trains. Soon, Camden began to seek Emily out in all activities of the day. Every day, he wanted to sit by her at circle time, do all center activities with her, and eat his lunch beside her. Eventually, Camden became upset if Emily chose to play with anyone else. His agitation increased to the point that he pushed other children to get near Emily or cried when he could not play with her. Eventually, Emily asked her teacher to place her in centers without Camden and find her another place to sit during circle time and lunch. Camden could not understand why Emily did not want to be with him all of the time during the school day.

Many children with ASD would like to have relationships with others, but struggle with the skills needed to initiate, develop, and maintain these relationships. Consider this situation that occurred when Kristen saw her teacher out shopping with her daughter, Anna. As soon as Kristen spotted her teacher, she ran up, greeting them, "What's up cats?" Before any introductions could be made, Kristen leaned into Anna, and within an inch of Anna's face, started a never-ending stream of questions such as "Will you be my friend?" "Do you want to be friends?" "Say, yes! Say, yes!" "Did you say yes?" Anna's response was to lean back into the grocery cart, with her muscles tense and her eyes wide open looking at her mom. Apparently, not noticing any discomfort, Kristen persisted with such questions as "Are we gonna hang out tonight?" "What are you doing after this?" Although Kristen is extremely eager to make friends, she wants to dominate the conversation and only talk about her own interests. Her overbearing manner and disregard of the responses of her communication partners cause great difficulty in social relationships with her peers.

CHARACTERISTIC
Individuals With ASD Typically Like Routines and May Have Significant Anxiety About Changes in Their Environment

Rigid adherence to routines is practically impossible in our fast-moving, ever-changing society. Some children with ASD respond to change with rocking, flapping their hands, jumping repetitively, or engaging in other recurring physical actions. Although these stereotypic motor movements or ritualistic routines sometimes occur for the sensory stimulation they provide, other times they occur as a result of frustration or anxiety associated with changes in the environment or disruption of routines.

Other children on the spectrum might resist change through loud, repetitive refusals or obstinate protesting. Still others might engage in persistent questioning about reasons for the change or even irrational negotiations to keep things the same.

When these resisting behaviors occur, social interactions can become awkward and uncomfortable. Typically developing children can feel tentative and uncertain about interacting, perhaps even unwilling to initiate any interaction. Even adults can be perplexed by these behaviors and tentative about approaching children who are resistant to change.

Ryan was interested in and fascinated by robots. He became skilled at creating robot-like figures from cardboard and aluminum foil. Two neighborhood children came over to play and within a few minutes, Ryan told them, "To build a robot, you must use the rectangular pieces that are covered with foil for the legs, then a rectangular bigger piece for the body. When those pieces are in place, then we can get the rectangular pieces for the arms." Ryan built a robot in the way he created all of his robots and any attempts by the other boys to create robots differently were stopped by Ryan's loud and increasingly agitated tone of voice. Ryan's insistence on following his ritual assembly of the robot in a regimented way, as well as his inappropriate comments and expectations of conformity, led to an unsuccessful interaction with his neighborhood friends.

CHARACTERISTIC

Individuals With ASD May Focus on Specific, Sometimes Irrelevant Details, Possibly to a Degree That May Result in Undergeneralizing and/or Overgeneralizing and/or Even Prevent Complete Understanding of a Concept or Situation

Imagine trying to interpret the actions of others by focusing on only one feature of their face or by noticing only gestures with the hands or arms. For example, raised eyebrows might indicate that a person is surprised or it could suggest that the person is offended. A person who is focusing only on the raised eyebrows could easily misread the situation. Consider the message implied by a pointed index finger. Depending on such factors as facial expression, muscle tension, and direction of the point, the meaning could be "Listen to this," "Come here," "Sit there," "Don't do that!" or "Look there!" It is easy to understand why concentrating only on the pointed finger could lead to misinterpreted communications.

Consider this situation. In the middle of a generally successful school year, Ian suddenly announced to his teacher that he didn't want to go to P.E. any more.

This was particularly puzzling because the coach was a terrific, positive, and accommodating P.E. teacher. At first, Ian was reluctant to explain why he didn't want to go; however, after a number of conversations, he finally admitted that he didn't want to go to P.E. because the coach might hit him. Mystified, Ian's teacher and the coach discussed every possible explanation for this inexplicable claim. Finally, the coach remembered ending a recent class with a series of celebratory fist bumps. Seeing fist bumps through Ian's eyes, it was easy to conclude that he only noticed the coach's fist contacting another fist. It is likely that Ian did not notice the happy facial expressions and approving tone of voice that accompanied the fist bumps.

CHARACTERISTIC

Individuals With ASD May be Hypersensitive or Hyposensitive and Thus React Atypically to Input From the Five Traditional Senses (Sight, Hearing, Touch, Smell, and Taste) as Well as the Vestibular and Kinesthetic Senses

Getting along with others involves going places in groups. Such sensitivity to changes in the environment, particularly with big settings and large numbers of people, can interfere with opportunities for children with ASD to enjoy social interactions.

Max began attending gym at the start of the school year, and he often reminded his parents and teachers, "Wednesdays are gym days!" He set out his tennis shoes every Tuesday night in anticipation of gym class on Wednesdays. One day, Max refused to enter the gym and could not be persuaded by his teacher or the coach to come inside. When his teacher looked in the gym, she noticed that half the lights were off and the children were watching a video. Max said the lights made his eyes "squinty" and the video noise sounded like "scratching on a wet window." His oversensitivity made it impossible for him to enjoy watching the video with his classmates.

CHARACTERISTIC

Individuals With ASD Might Demonstrate Predominantly Concrete Thinking and Thus Make Literal Interpretations of Statements and Situations

Literal interpretations can interfere with understanding the true meaning of a communication. Such limited understanding certainly affects social interactions. Most children with ASD have great difficulty with figurative language such as "Hold your horses," "He's in the doghouse," "It's raining cats and dogs," or

"That's a piece of cake." Unable to determine the real message from the context of the situation, they will look for the horses, house, cats, dogs, or cake.

Maurice's teacher was reading a story to the class about ice-skating. She decided to start the lesson with a simulation. She put two pieces of paper on the carpet, stepped on them, and pretended to skate by gliding over the carpet. She offered the other children a chance to try, but Maurice stayed at the table by himself with a puzzled look on his face. He explained to her in a firm tone that the paper and carpet were not ice skates and a skating rink. Maurice interpreted the story literally and, to him, there was no ice-skating rink, no skates to put on, and no reason for him to join his teacher and friends.

CHARACTERISTIC
Children With ASD Could Have Executive Functioning Challenges Such as an Impaired Ability to Initiate Tasks, Difficulty Making Transitions, and an Inability to Organize Complex Tasks

Children who have an impaired ability to initiate are at a disadvantage in social interactions. They are limited in their capacity to begin a communication exchange and unskilled in asserting themselves to ask for a turn in a game or other play situations.

Every day at recess, the second graders spent most of their time drawing with chalk on the asphalt. Although Kevin liked to draw, he walked around the perimeter of the group, watching the others. He made comments about their drawings, but didn't direct those comments to any individuals. Most of his comments were quiet and couldn't be heard by the other second graders. Whenever prompted by his teachers, Kevin would participate in drawing pictures. With help, he would ask others for different colors of chalk. However, on days that his teachers didn't prompt, he would revert to walking around the edge of the group.

Typical children watch and learn many of the unwritten and unspoken rules of initiating social interaction. Children with ASD miss many of these rules, as they don't carefully observe the interactions of others. Rather than wait to initiate interaction at a natural pause, some children with ASD will burst into a situation in an awkward way.

At lunch, Jenna and Melanie were sitting across from each other talking about their favorite TV shows. Erin brought her lunch tray over, squeezed in beside Jenna, and interrupted their conversation. Erin blurted out loudly, "I have a new salamander! It's an amphibian with trichromatic color vision that it uses to track its prey." As you can imagine, with such a blunt initiation and no transition to another topic, the conversation just stopped.

Each child with ASD will have some combination of these characteristics and each child will be unique. Our next chapter will look at general strategies for teaching social skills to children with ASD. In future chapters, we will present ideas for the use of games and other activities to help address the social challenges of children with ASD.

In the next chapter, we'll briefly discuss the most important methods of teaching children with autism. We'll begin with a brief description of Applied Behavior Analysis (ABA) and a few important terms and concepts. In Chapter 3, we'll describe some other important strategies and methodologies designed for teaching children with autism. Whenever possible, our examples will be related to teaching social skills.

In later chapters, we'll describe our framework as a way to blend many of these teaching approaches into fun and engaging games and activities. In this framework, we will present ways to take into consideration the many strengths and unique characteristics of children with autism.

CHAPTER 2

Essential ABA Principles for Teaching Social Skills

We believe that the best way to teach social skills is to base instruction on principles of Applied Behavior Analysis (ABA). These principles are rules or laws that can be used to explain, predict, and change behavior (Alberto & Troutman, 2013). Many studies recommend the use of ABA in teaching children with ASD (Lovaas, 1987; McEachin, Smith, & Lovaas, 1993; National Research Council, 2001; New York State Department of Health, 1999; Schreibman, 2005).

An understanding of ABA gives us the tools to examine the social behaviors of children with ASD by observing, labeling, and measuring the behaviors. Once we have good information, then we can arrange the environment to increase and strengthen the behaviors that are effective and productive. ABA also gives us the tools to decrease, weaken, or eliminate behaviors that interfere with development of social relationships. In the scenarios that follow, we've included specific strategies that were used to help develop social skills. These strategies are further discussed in the next two chapters.

Case Study: Jake

Although Jake could say the names of many of his favorite toys, he showed little interest in using this language to request toys from other children. He liked to play with toys, but he only played with them by himself. Even if another child had his favorite toy of the moment, he would not approach the other child to engage in play, request a turn, or even take the toy. Instead, he might rock and moan or even cry. These unproductive whining behaviors occurred 6 or 7 times a day. Unless given toys, Jake would engage in these behaviors for more than 15 minutes at a time.

Jake's teachers labeled the target behavior as "requesting a toy from a peer," and by collecting data, determined that Jake engaged in this skill less than one time per day. To increase his requesting behavior, they arranged teaching sessions around some of Jake's favorite items, including his musical top, See & Say™, and LEGOs™. Placing those toys on a table, just out of Jake's reach, they waited for him to move his hands toward one of them. As soon as he attempted to reach the item, his teachers placed a hand on the item and directed him to say the name of the item. As soon as he said the name of the item, his teacher would quickly give him an opportunity to play with it. Rather than reaching, having the toy blocked, and then making a request, Jake quickly learned that it was more efficient to say the name of the toy as a request. Once Jake was consistently requesting toys from an adult, his teachers arranged for two of his friends to sit at a table with Jake, holding his favorite toys until he asked for them. In this contrived setting, the friends immediately gave Jake the toys he requested. Next, the teachers arranged for Jake's friends to play with his toys on the carpet. They prompted Jake to approach the boys and ask for toys. Within a few days, Jake began going to the carpet area independently and asking his friends for his favorite toys. As he became more consistent with this, his teachers increased the demands by requiring him to say phrases such as "Can I have the top?" or "Can I play with the LEGOs™?"

In the meantime, Jake's undesired behaviors (rocking and moaning and crying) decreased to 1 or 2 times a day. And as soon as Jake began these behaviors, a teacher could point to the carpet and Jake would get up to go ask for his toys. Later in the semester, Jake's teachers used similar teaching procedures to help Jake take turns with toys and share toys with other children.

Jake's teachers were using principles of ABA. First, they identified and labeled the target behavior as "requesting a toy" and considered Jake's *motivation*, setting up opportunities for Jake to get what he wanted by performing the skill Jake's teachers wanted him to learn. They put his favorite toys just out of Jake's reach (contriving motivation), provided a direction with a *model* (such as "say top") as a *prompt* (an extra stimulus designed to help Jake learn what to do). When Jake said "top," they provided *positive reinforcement* (a stimulus designed to increase the probability that Jake would repeat the behavior in the future). As Jake became proficient at saying "top," they *shaped* (reinforced successive steps toward a final behavior) the behavior by requiring better requests such as "Can I have the top, please?" To get Jake to make the requests independently, they *faded* (gradually decreased and then eliminated) the prompts. Once Jake was comfortable making requests for toys from his teachers, they transferred *stimulus control* (arranged for Jake to perform the behavior with other children instead of just the teacher). When Jake began to moan or rock, his teachers first tried to use an *extinction* procedure (withholding reinforcement) to decrease or eliminate this unproductive behavior. They ignored the behaviors (by withholding attention), but quickly found that Jake continued to moan and rock and then would eventually cry. They coupled this extinction procedure with a *modeling* procedure by arranging for a peer to approach another peer to ask loudly for the toy. This attracted Jake's attention and, as he saw the model receiving reinforcement (getting the toy), he then went to request the item for himself.

Case Study: Chrissie

Chrissie came to school everyday and followed the classroom routines precisely. When her teachers and peers greeted her, she always responded with "Hi." She listened to the teacher, worked at her desk, ate lunch, and turned her work in on time. However, unless prompted, Chrissie rarely interacted with others. Her teachers used principles of ABA to teach Chrissie to initiate conversations with her peers. First, they considered motivation by talking with Chrissie and finding out her favorite things (a reinforcement survey). Chrissie loved Justin Bieber and listened to his music at home every chance she got. However, there were not many opportunities to listen to music during the school day, so her teachers explained that she would be able to listen to Justin's music with friends three times a day. Chrissie was eager to hear how this could happen! The three times were designated as (a) the last 10 minutes of homeroom, (b) the last 10 minutes of lunch, and (c) the last 10 minutes before going home. Chrissie's objective was to invite a friend to meet her in the speech room at the designated times. To help Chrissie develop the skills needed to ask friends, her teacher first developed a task analysis of the first step of the skill and made the visual support in Figure 1 for Chrissie to use to invite a friend.

Next, her teacher modeled the target behavior. To set up the situation, she asked two girls to sit at a table in the lunchroom and talk. Asking Chrissie to watch, the teacher waited for a pause in the girls' conversation and then asked the girls if they would like to come with Chrissie to hear some music by Justin Bieber. Over several days, the teacher modeled this, each time letting Chrissie and her peers listen to music.

When it was Chrissie's turn to initiate by herself, the teacher used priming at the beginning of the day. She reminded Chrissie of the upcoming opportunity to hear music when she invited her friends to come.

Inviting a Friend to Hear Music

Step 1. Approach your friends and wait for a person to look up at you or wait for a pause in the conversation

Step 2. Say something like, "I get to listen to some Justin Bieber music today at the end of lunch. Would you like to come with me?"

Step 3. Wait for the person to respond.

Step 4. Make a choice:

If the person says, "yes," then say something like "Great! I'll meet you in the speech room at 11:45."	If the person says, "no," then say, "Thanks, anyway. Maybe another time!"

Figure 1. Visual support for Chrissie.

Chrissie's experience acted as positive reinforcement, not only because Chrissie was happy listening to the Justin Bieber music, but also because at the end of the session she said, "I want to ask another friend." Within a few weeks, Chrissie seemed comfortable asking friends to come listen to music, but she was still not carrying on conversations with her friends. Setting another target objective, her teacher made a choice board (see Figure 2) of possible questions she could ask her friends at the end of each song. Chrissie used a self-management chart (see Figure 3) to keep track of the number of questions she asked each day. Her teacher set up an incentive for Chrissie to ask 10 questions each day (about three or four questions each session). If Chrissie met that goal, she would earn an opportunity to download a new Justin Bieber song.

Chrissie's teacher was shaping or reinforcing successive approximations of the complex skill of conversing with others. It took many weeks of practice to gradually teach the skills of Chrissie's task analysis (see Figure 4 for a list of the desired skills for Chrissie).

Jake and Chrissie's stories provide a brief introduction to a few of the concepts of ABA. There are many, many ways to implement principles of ABA in teaching. In the following sections, we will expand on these terms and then highlight some research-based practices for teaching social skills to children with ASD.

Choice Board

In the music room, you can ask such questions as:

What song would you like to hear next?
What are your favorite facts about Justin Bieber?
Do you want to look at some pictures of Justin Bieber?
What are your favorite Justin Bieber songs?
Do you have any other favorite music?

Figure 2. Choice board for Chrissie.

Questions Asked Each Day

Monday	Tuesday	Wednesday	Thursday	Friday
Question 1	Question 1	Question 1	Question 1	Question 1
Question 2	Question 2	Question 2	Question 2	Question 2
Question 3	Question 3	Question 3	Question 3	Question 3
Question 4	Question 4	Question 4	Question 4	Question 4
Question 5	Question 5	Question 5	Question 5	Question 5

AWESOME **Congratulations!**
25 questions = New Justin Bieber Song!

Figure 3. Token economy for Chrissie.

- Approaching a peer and waiting for the peer to look up or pause
- Intiating a question or statement when the peer looks at her or pauses
- Asking questions from the choice board
- Listening to answers of friends
- Adding a comment relevant to the answers of friends
- Maintaining a conversation for five or six exchanges
- Ending the conversation politely

Figure 4. Task analysis for Chrissie.

The Formal Definition of ABA

ABA is the process of systematically applying interventions based upon the principles of learning theory to improve socially significant behaviors to a meaningful degree, and to demonstrate that the interventions employed are responsible for the improvement in behavior (Baer, Wolf, & Risley, 1968). The ABA process includes examining behavior by focusing on the environmental events that come before and after the behavior. This is often described as collecting information on the ABCs of behavior analysis—that is, we analyze the antecedents (A) to a behavior, the behavior (B) itself, and the consequences (C) to the behavior. We then manipulate the antecedents and consequences systematically, resulting in changes in socially significant behavior. The effectiveness of ABA has been confirmed by many experimental studies and can be applied in a variety of settings and with many individuals, including children with ASD.

In this book, we'll discuss how we can teach new social skills such as using polite words to make requests, looking where others are looking, commenting on things in the environment, and conversing with others. We also can strengthen, improve, or increase social skills that are already in the child's repertoire. For example, we can teach children skills such as using longer sentences or increasing the number of verbal exchanges. ABA helps us maintain the effective social skills that children have. For example, once a child is using a skill such as asking a friend to play, we can teach the child to continue doing it even if the friend doesn't say yes every time. We can use ABA to help children generalize their social skills or transfer them to other situations. For example, if the child learns to share items with others at school, ABA can help us teach the child to share with friends at home. And ABA helps us reduce interfering behaviors such as repetitive, self-stimulating behavior, socially disruptive behavior such as blurting out in class, or socially inappropriate behavior such as ignoring a conversation partner. The following ABA principles and concepts are important to understand, as they will give us the tools to accomplish the important skills we've listed above.

Motivation

Understanding the motivation of children involves observing and investigating their behavior. Generally, children want to meet their survival needs (e.g., food, drink, opportunity to move). As they grow, they want attention, praise, other tangible items, activities, privileges, and relationships with other people.

Reinforcer or preference assessments range from asking children what they like to observing what they prefer to do when given free time. In addition, when interviewing or observing, it is important to learn about that child's motivating operations (the conditions that alter the value of the effectiveness of consequences and help us understand what children want and don't want). Two conditions that affect the value of consequences that are potential reinforcers are those of satiation (a large amount of the potential reinforcer has been recently available) and deprivation (the potential reinforcer has not recently been available). With satiation, we often notice a decrease in the strength or frequency of a behavior that precedes the consequence, and with deprivation, we often notice an increase in the strength or frequency of the behavior preceding the consequence.

CAPTURING OR CONTRIVING MOTIVATION

In teaching, we can sometimes capture motivation; that is, we can take advantage of what is currently interesting to the child by providing what the child wants immediately after the child performs the target behavior. For example, if the child is interested in playing computer games and the target behavior is to make a polite request, then we can set up a teaching situation where a period of time to play on the computer is provided immediately after the child says something like, "Could I please play now?"

We sometimes have to work to contrive motivation by manipulating situations in which the value of the reinforcer changes. If a child has free access to computer games at home and is satiated, playing on a computer at school may have less value. However, a child who hasn't been able to play in quite a while (thus, has been deprived) might be very interested in the opportunity to play.

For some children, we may have to work to expand their reinforcers. By pairing neutral stimuli with powerful reinforcers, those stimuli can take on reinforcing value. For example, initially "high fives" may not act as reinforcers, but, when paired with positive attention, they become social reinforcers. Consider the case of Lauren, who had no interest in taking a walk with a peer. After each work session, her teachers set up an opportunity to take a 5-minute walk with another child. At the end of the walk, Lauren and the peer were provided an opportunity to watch a 5-minute cartoon. After several weeks, the walk itself, without the cartoon, was just as reinforcing as watching the cartoon.

To work effectively with children who have learning and behavioral challenges, we need to be constantly aware of their motivating operations. This may be as simple as establishing positive relationships with children by spending time with them, doing things they like to do, and talking about things they like to discuss. These children may already value attention and praise, but many others may need tangible reinforcers such as activities, privileges, prizes, and food. For those children, it is especially important that the teacher's attention and praise become associated (paired) with tangible reinforcers. Sometimes referred to as the process of conditioning ourselves as reinforcers, it is important to pair ourselves with things that children really like.

For example, when arriving at a school to play games with a group of children, the authors found the children engaged in highly reinforcing sensory activities such as swinging and spinning. Noticing how much fun the kids were having, the authors were concerned about making a transition to a table game. The teachers gathered the children together to take a bathroom break and then directed them to come to the table. The children reluctantly came to the table; however, when they saw bags of pretzels and candy, they immediately became interested in what these strangers planned to do. For the first 10 minutes, each child was rewarded with plenty of praise, attention, and edibles. Before the end of the first game, no edibles were needed and praise and attention from the authors were acting as reinforcers.

We must work continuously to see things through the eyes of our children. When we understand what they want, need and enjoy, we can use that information to help expand their social world.

Positive Reinforcement

Positive reinforcement is the ABA principle that describes the idea that people usually repeat behaviors that result in pleasant consequences. The term *positive reinforcer* describes the consequence that increases the chance that the behavior will be repeated in the future. When a behavior is reinforced, the child is likely to repeat it so that the good things that happened will happen again.

Remember that candy, toys, attention, and sensory activities are not always positive reinforcers. The only consequences that are considered positive reinforcers are ones that cause behavior to be repeated or strengthened. Even though we assume that these are pleasant consequences, they may act as reinforcers for the behavior of some children and not for others. For example, if a child's action is followed by an M&M™, but the child doesn't like M&Ms™, the action is not likely to be repeated.

Understanding the principle of positive reinforcement is helpful in understanding how children learn. For example, if a child learns that asking for a desired toy results in getting an opportunity to play with that toy, the child is likely to ask again. However, it is also possible that a child could learn that grabbing a toy from another child results in an opportunity to play with the toy. In both cases, the opportunity to play with the toy acts as a positive reinforcer. In the first case, the child is likely to ask again; in the second case, the child is likely to grab again. We know that getting the toy to play with after asking is an effective reinforcer for asking only if, in the future, the child asks for the toy.

To use positive reinforcement to teach a skill, we arrange for positive reinforcers to occur immediately and consistently after the behavior we want to increase. So, we do our best to ensure that children get opportunities to play with toys after asking (and not after grabbing).

SCHEDULES OF REINFORCEMENT

When using positive reinforcement as a tool to teach, it can be provided continuously—that is, provided immediately after every single time the targeted behavior occurs. Or, it can be provided intermittently—in other words, only after some of the times the behavior occurs.

In the beginning, it is important to arrange for reinforcement regularly and continuously, if possible. However, because that is not always realistic, we aim to manage the consequences as consistently as possible. To continue with the example above, if children learn that the majority of times they ask for the toy, they get it, and the majority of times they grab the toy, they lose it, they eventually find asking to be the most efficient and effective way of getting the toy.

Intermittent reinforcement can actually strengthen behaviors. So, if periodically a child grabs a toy and gets a nice, long opportunity to play, it is likely that the child might grab it again. If that happens regularly enough, grabbing may become that child's most efficient and effective way of getting a toy.

Perhaps you can already see the value in using intermittent reinforcement to increase and strengthen target behaviors. We might, for example, want to teach children to persist in asking friends to play, even though they won't be able to play every time. If the reward is powerful enough (the friend plays) and can be delivered regularly (e.g., after every third correct occurrence of a behavior), the child learns to keep trying. In some cases, if the reward is powerful and delivered on a variable schedule (e.g., after the first occurrence, then the third occurrence, then the fifth occurrence, then the third occurrence), the child learns to persist the same way gamblers keep putting quarters in a slot machine.

When we are trying to teach persistence, we try to use a powerful reward with a variable schedule. We make sure the reward is provided often enough. Otherwise, the schedule of reinforcement becomes too thin and the child gives up because the reward hardly ever happens. To keep track, we report the schedule as an average. In the previous example, we used a variable ratio 3 (VR3) because the reward was delivered on an average of every 3 correct responses (i.e., $1 + 3 + 5 + 3 = 12$, divided by $4 = 3$).

Pairing

Pairing is a principle that describes the idea that things that happen closely in time become associated with each other. For example, when a baby cries and a mother appears, the baby learns to associate the cry with the mother. To teach, we often present things together. So, for example, to teach a child to follow the direction, "Sit down," we pair it with helping the child to sit while we say it.

We can use pairing to help children learn the value of social reinforcement. If children aren't responding to praise and attention, we can start by rewarding the child with a cracker or small pieces of candy. To pair the treat with social reinforcement, it is best to present the social reward (verbal praise such as "Good!" or positive action such as a high five) immediately before handing over the treat. Remember the case of Lauren and the opportunity to walk with a friend before watching a cartoon? Initially, the meaningful reinforcer was the opportunity to watch the cartoon; however, after pairing the two together, the walk itself became reinforcing. In either case, through pairing, the previously ineffective social reward becomes associated with and takes on the value of the more effective reward (the treat or the cartoon).

Reinforcers are called primary when they initially, on their own, increase the chance the behavior will occur again. Examples of primary reinforcers may include food, sensory activities, or, for some children, attention. Secondary reinforcers are those that initially have no effect on the behavior, but eventually (after pairing with primary reinforcers) increase the chance the behavior will occur again. For example, very young children have no understanding that a sticker or happy face is a good thing. They come to respond to stickers and happy faces only after they become associated with primary reinforcers such as food or toys.

Using tokens for reinforcement can be a very helpful and powerful teaching aid. Tokens can be stickers, coins, points, tickets, or anything else that represents a reinforcer. Token reinforcement is often delivered by setting up a token economy. This is just a system where the tokens are accumulated and then exchanged for a more tangible reward. A simple economy can consist of a token (happy face) chart such as the one in Figure 5. To use this, we move a token (secondary reinforcer) from the bottom of the chart to the top to provide a reinforcer for a behavior. In this case, when three tokens are earned, they are exchanged for a reward (hopefully a positive reinforcer). As in other forms of reinforcement, the consequence isn't really a reinforcer unless it is increasing the chance that the behavior will be repeated in the future.

In this example, the teacher either moves the happy face or directs the child to move it. A "Wow!" token represents the positive reinforcer. A matching "Wow!" token can be placed on a bag of chips, on a swing set, or on whatever the reward is to be. Another way to use this chart is to select from among the

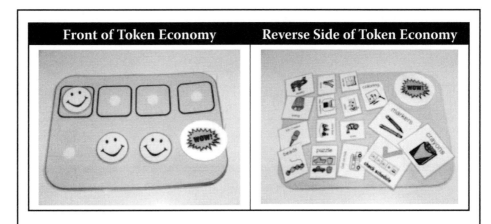

| Front of Token Economy | Reverse Side of Token Economy |

Figure 5. Token economy chart.

reinforcing activities that are stuck with Velcro™ to the back of the happy face chart. In other cases, children can have point charts or banks that allow them to manage their tokens and purchase rewards from a menu or classroom store.

We also use pairing to help children learn the value of interacting with people. When social attention and praise are not enough to interest children in interacting with others, we pair people with things the children like. For example, if a child particularly enjoys puzzles, we can increase the opportunities for her to do puzzles with others and decrease the times she works puzzles alone. Eventually, the enjoyment of doing puzzles becomes associated with people. The joint activities have to be positive though, because if every puzzle session with others results in crying or arguing, the negative experience is what becomes associated with people.

It is especially important to be aware of the preferences of children with ASD. They often have unique patterns of likes and dislikes and these can be quite strong.

Modeling

Modeling involves providing a demonstration of behavior for the child to imitate. Modeling generally works because children see others reinforced for a behavior and act because there is a potential reinforcer for imitating the behavior. Modeling can be used to prompt simple responses, such as clapping, as well as complex behaviors like taking turns with peers.

Some children with ASD may find it difficult to respond to long, detailed verbal descriptions and instructions of what we want them to do. Modeling capitalizes on the visual strengths of many children with ASD by allowing them to watch a demonstration and then imitate a response.

Modeling can be particularly useful when children are anxious about trying something new. For example, if a child is uncomfortable asking a friend to play, we can arrange for another friend to make the request, allowing the child to watch while the two other friends interact. Seeing the request result in a positive play experience can encourage the child to try the next time.

In the natural environment, many typical children imitate models for the social reinforcement. Don't forget that some children with ASD need primary reinforcement specifically for imitating models, as they don't always value social reinforcement.

Shaping

The process of shaping involves providing reinforcement of small steps for successive approximations of a desired behavior. This means identifying a behavior, breaking it into steps, and systematically reinforcing the steps of the behavior that shift closer to the actual final behavior. To shape the behavior of maintaining eye contact, we might first reinforce a child for orienting toward the teacher. Next, we would reinforce the behavior of looking in the teacher's face, and finally of looking into the teacher's eyes.

To teach a complex social skill such as conversing with others, it's possible to start by reinforcing one step of the behavior, such as saying, "Hi, how are you?" Once that behavior is mastered, the next step might be reinforcing asking and answering a question about favorite movies. A third step might be reinforcing a conversation with five exchanges, and a last step might be reinforcing ending the conversation with an appropriate phrase such as "Nice talking with you."

Prompting and Fading

A prompt is an additional cue or hint that is provided in order to help a child give a correct response. Different types of prompts include: physical prompts (e.g., hand over hand guidance), gesture prompts (e.g., pointing, hand movements), visual prompts (e.g., picture cues, written text), model prompts (e.g., demonstrations), directions (e.g., explanations, instructions), and positional prompts (e.g., placement of correct item).

Prompts are especially helpful in teaching a new skill with the process called errorless teaching. In this case, we provide prompts immediately so that the child makes the correct response every time. For example, if we want a child to approach and say "Hi!" to another child, we would physically guide the child over to the friend and say, "Say 'Hi!'" to the child. Errorless teaching may also be called "most-to-least (MTL) prompting," as it begins with the highest level prompt necessary to ensure success. In addition to being effective in teaching a new skill, MTL prompting is also useful when we want the child to practice a skill without making any errors.

In least-to-most (LTM) prompting, we wait for the child to make an attempt. If the attempt is incorrect, we provide the least amount of prompting necessary for the child to succeed. This prompting hierarchy is valuable when children become "prompt dependent"—that is, they begin to wait for a prompt before attempting a task. In this case, we let the child initiate a response and provide just enough prompting to ensure success.

To summarize the advantages and disadvantages: In MTL prompting, children make very few errors, but potentially become prompt dependent. In LTM prompting, children learn to initiate responses, but sometimes errors can interfere with or delay learning.

Fading is the systematic and gradual removal of prompts. After teaching the skill with a verbal prompt ("say, 'Hi Will!'"), fade to a gesture or visual prompt to help the child to approach and greet Will. To keep learning without errors, we would use enough prompts to ensure the child performs the behavior as expected and fade the prompts gradually so the child experiences success all along the way. The behavior is considered mastered when the child can perform it independently, without prompts.

Whether using MTL or LTM prompting, the goal is eventually to fade all of the prompts so the child is performing the task independently. It is important to fade prompts gradually because the child's response may decrease or stop completely when prompts are removed too quickly.

Task Analysis

A task analysis involves taking a complex skill and breaking it down into smaller, teachable steps. The task analysis should be based on the child's individual needs and the child's language and motor abilities. The specific behaviors and the sequence of behaviors that need to be completed in order to perform the target skill efficiently and effectively need to be determined.

It is important to validate (check for accuracy and relevance) the task analysis for effectiveness. To validate the task analysis "Inviting a Friend to Join a Play Activity" (see Figure 6), observe peers the same age as the child playing, consult with an expert in language development, and/or or ask a peer of the child to model how he would invite a friend to play with him. When necessary, use

---

Inviting a Friend to Join a Play Activity

1. Go get close to my friend and wait for the friend to look up.
2. Look at my friend.
3. Ask my friend to play with me.
4. Wait for my friend to answer.
5. If my friend says, "yes," say, "Ok! Let's go."
6. If my friend says, "no," or "not now," I can ask another friend or play by myself for a little while.

Figure 6. Task analysis for inviting a friend to join in play.

---

the information gained in the observation and consultations to rearrange the sequence or add missing steps.

Chaining

A complex skill may be broken down into a task analysis (list of smaller steps of the complex skill). When these steps are connected together, they form a behavioral chain. The teaching procedure in which reinforcement is provided for connecting these small steps of a more complex behavior in order is called chaining.

Once a task analysis is developed, we can use one of three ways to teach the task. The first is a forward chaining procedure. In this case, we teach the first step in the chain, provide reinforcement, and prompt the child through the remaining steps. We add steps one at a time until the child can perform all steps in the chain.

In the second, backward chaining, prompt the child through the initial steps in the chain. Then, teach the child to complete the final step in the chain and provide reinforcement for completing it. The second step to teach is the next-to-last step. When the child can perform the last two steps independently, add the next steps in the chain, one at a time, moving gradually toward the first step. Continue systematic instruction until all steps in the chain are mastered.

In the third process, total task presentation, we provide instruction in each step of the task analysis during every session. Initially, we provide prompts for all steps and gradually fade the prompts until the child can perform the entire task independently.

An advantage of total task presentation is that the child is receiving training on each step in the chain during every session. For some children, on some tasks, mastery may come quicker when seeing the whole task in context. However, for others, or on other tasks, tackling the whole task at once may be confusing.

Stimulus Control

One important aspect of teaching is to get children to perform skills reliably at certain times under certain circumstances. As behaviorists, we refer to this as getting behavior under stimulus control. There are four conditions to determine whether or not a behavior is under stimulus control. First, the behavior has to occur immediately when the stimulus is provided. Consider the example of a social skill such as giving a high five. A vertical, palm out hand is often meant to be a stimulus for a high five. If the behavior of giving a high five is under stimulus control, the child would immediately reach to slap hands with a person who has offered a hand in a high five position. Second, the behavior does not occur in the absence of the stimulus. Thus, the child wouldn't go around giving high fives if a person wasn't there. Third, the behavior doesn't occur in response to some other stimulus. In this case, the child would not give a high five when a person offers a hand in a handshaking position. And, lastly, no other behavior occurs in response to the stimulus. So, for example, the child would not respond with a handshaking position to a hand offered in a high five position.

Understanding the concept of stimulus control is very important when teaching social skills to children with ASD. We recommend that you first provide clear stimuli and teach appropriate or acceptable responses. Then, teach children how to recognize similar stimuli in the environment and respond in a similar manner.

Having good social skills requires the ability to learn what is acceptable, or expected in certain situations; in other words, a person has to notice aspects of the environment (stimuli) and then determine responses to those aspects that would be the typical responses of most people. Thus, we might first provide quite a bit of practice extending our hands and reinforcing expected responses (e.g., handshake to handshake position and high five to high five position). Then, we would arrange for other children and adults to come by offering similar greetings. Last, we would challenge children to respond to naturally occurring opportunities.

Generalization

Children with ASD often have trouble generalizing social skills. To help these children have successful social interactions, we often need thoughtful planning and systematic instruction to assist them in using their skills at different times, in different settings, and with different people. Mayer, Sulzer-Azaroff, and Wallace (2012) explained that the simplest way to promote generalization is to ask for it. For example, Alex learned to ask interesting questions about peers while playing the game "Get to Know You Bingo" in a small group focusing on social skills instruction. The teacher told Alex, "Remember how you learned the skill of asking your friends interesting questions about themselves during the game? You could also use that same skill while sitting across from your friend at lunch."

Another way to program for generalization is to teach sufficient stimulus and response examples (Mayer, Sulzer-Azaroff, & Wallace, 2012). Often, the more examples we teach, the more likely the behavior will generalize. For instance, when teaching a child to respond to a question like, "How are you today?" arrange for different people (teachers, peers, and family members) to ask him, and have them vary the question slightly (i.e., "How are you?" or "How are things going today?").

Sometimes, children with ASD overgeneralize behaviors. For example, Rodrick practiced raising his hand at school to get the teacher's attention and when he wanted to answer a question. When he was at home having dinner with his family, Rodrick's mom asked, "How was your day today?" Rodrick immediately raised his hand and waited for his mom to call on him. If overgeneralization occurs, the child may require additional instruction in discriminating when and where to perform the target behavior.

Extinction

Extinction occurs when reinforcement no longer follows a behavior, and there is a reduction in the future occurrence of the behavior as a result. Understanding the principle of extinction helps us realize why some previously mastered behaviors seem to disappear. For instance, it might be that a child learned to raise her hand in class to get attention. Initially, perhaps the teacher called on the child frequently, reinforcing the behavior with attention. If the teacher goes too many days without calling on the child, the child may quit raising her hand and begin blurting out to get attention. In this case, we would say the hand-raising behavior was extinguished.

We can use our understanding of this principle to extinguish behaviors that interfere with social relationships. However, to do this, we need to know what purpose the behavior serves. Many teachers have intended to use extinction by ignoring behaviors such as clowning around in class. Unfortunately, if attention from the teacher isn't the reinforcing consequence, withholding attention will not extinguish the behavior. It is highly likely the reinforcer maintaining clowning around in class is actually attention from classmates, not attention from the teacher. If this is the case, extinction will not work unless attention from classmates can be withheld. And that is quite difficult to do!

Extinction is more efficient when used in combination with reinforcement of other appropriate behaviors. So success is more likely if we can implement extinction by withholding the maintaining reinforcer and also provide positive reinforcement for an incompatible or competing behavior. To continue with the above example, we would ask the class not to laugh or react (withholding attention from classmates), while at the same time providing attention, praise, and privileges for on-task behavior (incompatible with clowning around).

Punishment

Punishment is another principle that explains why behaviors are sometimes eliminated or reduced. There are two types of punishment procedures. The first is called positive punishment, and it occurs when a behavior is reduced or eliminated as a result of a stimulus that followed it. For example, if a verbal reprimand to a child for interrupting class stops interruptions in the future, we can say the interrupting behavior was punished positively. This doesn't mean the consequence was positive, it just means that a stimulus was provided (rather than taken away). Anytime a stimulus results in a future decrease in behavior, we can say punishment occurred.

Even if a compliment reduces a future occurrence of a behavior, we can say that the compliment served as a punisher. For example, when Connor's teacher said (in front of the class), "Thanks, Connor, for turning in your homework on time!" Connor turned red and slid down in his seat. He didn't turn his homework in the next day and, when asked, said he was embarrassed by the teacher's compliment.

On the other hand, it is interesting to note that if a verbal reprimand serves as attention that the child likes, and the interrupting behavior increases in the future, then the behavior was reinforced. Just as candy, privileges, and praise are only reinforcers if they strengthen and increase behavior, verbal reprimands or other events are only punishers if they weaken or reduce behaviors in the future.

Negative punishment occurs when a behavior is reduced or eliminated as a result of a loss of positive events. As an opposite to positive punishment (where we provide a stimulus), in negative punishment, we take the stimulus away. If we take away attention, tangible items, or privileges, and the behavior is weakened or reduced, then we can say the behavior was negatively punished.

Time out is an example of negative punishment. It can best be described as time out from reinforcement. For example, consider a child who likes working a puzzle and reciting a movie script. To use time out to reduce reciting the movie script, taking the puzzle away for 30 seconds might serve as time-out-on-the-spot. This assumes that the puzzle was reinforcing and that the child stopped the scripting before the puzzle was returned.

Many times, we try to implement time out by removing a child from a group. If the child is acting out (yelling or hitting) during group play, it's possible that removing the child from the group might serve as time out from reinforcement. If the child stops yelling and hitting in future play sessions, the time out served as a punisher. However, if the child continues to yell or hit in groups, time out did not serve as a punisher. A likely reason is that the child did not find the group play reinforcing and perhaps even wanted to escape. In this case, we might even see an increase in future yelling and hitting.

With both positive and negative punishment, it is important to understand that the behavior decreases in the future. When we understand the concept of punishment, we can explain why some good behaviors go away. For example, it is possible that a child might say "hi" to a group of peers who then respond with lots of enthusiastic conversation. If that makes the child uncomfortable, the child might not say "hi" to a group again.

Using the concept of punishment to analyze behavior is often more useful than using it intentionally as a tool to reduce behaviors. Other than the use of mild verbal reprimands or short time-out-on-the-spot procedures, punishment creates a negative atmosphere that does not enhance social interactions.

Positive Behavior Supports

The practice of using Positive Behavior Supports (PBS; Horner, 2000) involves the systematic use of ABA principles to reduce problem behaviors by replacing them with productive, prosocial behaviors. We start with a functional behavior assessment (FBA), a process for defining target behavior(s) for change, collecting data, looking for patterns of behavior, and developing a hypothesis for "why" the behavior occurs (the function of the behavior). By gathering enough information about events that occur before the behavior (antecedents) and events following the behavior (consequences), we can often accurately predict when a problem behavior is likely to occur, and we can frequently agree on the consequences that are maintaining the problem behavior (see Figure 7). Then, in order to create an effective and efficient behavior intervention plan, we arrange the environment to make the problem behaviors inefficient and ineffective for whatever function the behavior is serving (O'Neill et al., 1997). Using the information from our FBA, we can focus on teaching children alternative or replacement behaviors that are more effective than engaging in problem behavior (Carr & Durand, 1985).

Antecedent	Behavior	Consequence	Possible Function
Derrick is playing with Abbie's favorite light-up toy on the carpet	Abbie grabs the toy from Derrick	Abbie plays with the toy	To get (obtain) her favorite toy

Figure 7. FBA data entry for Abbie.

The functions of behaviors include

- *attention* from others;
- *escape* from an activity, task, or person;
- to *obtain* items such as food, toys, or activities; and
- *automatic reinforcement* to produce an internally pleasing stimulus or stop an aversive stimulus from occurring.

When completing the FBA process, we investigate these behavior factors like a detective working to solve the mystery of understanding why a person engages in a particular behavior under certain conditions. Once the hypothesis is developed, we can use a functional analysis to manipulate the antecedents and consequences in an attempt to confirm the hypothesis. When the hypothesis seems fairly certain, a Positive Behavior Support plan can be developed. This plan includes using ABA strategies to address any skill deficits and to reduce problem behavior by teaching alternative behaviors that serve the same function as the problem behavior served.

For example, consider the case of a child who grabs toys from a peer. It is likely that the function is to obtain the toy. (However, until an FBA is completed, we may not know whether the function is to get the toy or to get attention from an adult who intervenes when this happens.) But, assuming the function is to grab the toy, a PBS plan would include strategies (like the ones described next) to teach the child to ask for the toy. Again, assuming that the reason the child grabs is to get the toy, asking for the toy serves the same function as grabbing the toy.

The next chapter provides a detailed listing of the various strategies that can be used to teach social skills to children with ASD with emphasis on those used in the games and activities later in the book.

Strategies and Methodologies Useful for Teaching Social Skills

The strategies in the following pages will be used throughout the games and activities that are described later in the book. Later, they will be used in the instructions for teaching 10 specific social skills. *Naturalistic teaching methods* embed instruction into routine and child-led activities. They use naturally occurring contexts to develop responsiveness, initiating, turn-taking, and joint attention and use logical consequences that are related to the current environment. The category of *controlled presentations* includes methods that are adult-directed, fast-paced, and focused on teaching component parts of complex tasks. These strategies often include repetitive practice and direct instruction on isolated skills. *Cognitive interventions* include focus on teaching children the connections between thinking, feeling, and behaving. *Environmental engineering approaches* are those that focus on arranging and manipulating aspects of the environment to assist in success. They include supports that help create a sense of predictability and set the stage for communicating clear expectations to children.

Naturalistic Teaching Methods

ACTIVITY-BASED INSTRUCTION

Activity-based instruction (ABI) describes the use of systematic teaching that is embedded in highly engaging play activities and common routines that are meaningful and interesting to the child (Bricker & Cripe, 1992). For example, to teach the skill of requesting, we would create play sessions with materials that the child wants and use prompting and reinforcement strategies to teach her to ask for those things. Perhaps we might put out a train track, but keep all of the trains and accessories out of reach of the children. In initial instruction, we might offer one toy, and ask, "Train?" When the child says (or attempts to say "train"), we provide the train and a reinforcing comment such as, "Sure! You can have the train!"

As the play routines develop, we can wait for children to initiate requests themselves. In addition, we can create opportunities for increased language interactions by asking questions such as "Which car do you want?" (the engine or the caboose), "Where do you want the train?" (on the bridge or under it), or "How many cars do you want?" (one, two, or three).

In ABI, we use natural stimuli and consequences, present skills in sequence with other skills as they would typically occur, and promote independent, child-initiated behaviors (Noonan & McCormick, 1993). Thus, we prompt and reinforce sharing, taking turns, and saying "thank you" all within the context of play. In addition, good ABI is implemented through the day, perhaps during several different play sessions as well as at snack time, lunchtime, or even arrival and departure. Implementing instruction across contexts increases the probability that the child will generalize the skill across environments.

Activity-based instruction is also a valuable teaching tool because it can target several objectives for one child. In addition, one activity can create a situation to work on different skills for different children. Figure 8 shares some steps for using ABI, along with examples to guide you through the steps.

CHOICE-MAKING INTERVENTIONS

Providing choices for children with autism can increase motivation (Koegel, Singh, & Keogel (2010) and decrease challenging behaviors (Carter, 2001). When it is difficult to motivate a child to do a difficult or unpreferred task, we can offer a choice of reinforcers (e.g., "Do you want the ball or the train?"). Choices such as this can provide an incentive for the child to work. Even offering a choice between two work tasks (e.g., "Do you want to do math or reading?") has been shown to decrease problem behavior.

Steps for Using ABI

1. Pick target objectives for each child such as:
   a. Ali—make requests using colors and share a toy
   b. Charlie—take turns in conversations, describe objects with two adjectives
   c. Denise—answer "who" and "where" questions

2. Create opportunities for teaching, including providing highly motivating, engaging activities as well as naturally occurring routines throughout the day. For example:
   a. Give everyone paper and a paintbrush, but keep all the brushes, paint jars, markers, and crayons out of reach of the children. Say something like, "You can make a picture with some or all of these things! There are markers for drawing, paint and paintbrushes for painting, and crayons for coloring. You can ask for a turn with any of these, so now what would you like?"
   b. When appropriate:
      i. Prompt and reinforce Ali for requesting a turn with each color of paint, and requesting a turn with each color of marker.
      ii. Ask Charlie follow-up questions such as, "Which paint brush do you want?" (i.e., the big orange one or the small blue one)
      iii. Ask Denise follow-up questions such as, "Who has the green paint?" and "Where's the paper?"

3. Reinforce appropriate answers with social praise, positive comments, and natural consequences. Natural consequences can include reinforcing language such as "Sure. Thanks for asking so nicely!" and "Wow! Now you can paint with blue!"
4. Create opportunities throughout the day (in different activities, settings, routines) and with different people (peers and teachers).

Figure 8. Sample steps for using ABI.

Instead of participating in small-group activities, Tarique would often wander around the room. Tarique remained unmotivated to engage in the tasks even when his teacher provided individualized instructions to get started. His teacher found success in offering him choices for something in each required activity. For example, as shown in Figure 9, she directed Tarique to complete the word wall activity, but gave him a choice of writing implement.

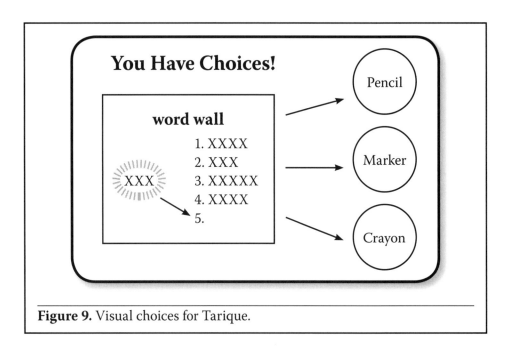

Figure 9. Visual choices for Tarique.

INCIDENTAL TEACHING

Incidental teaching is a naturalistic teaching procedure, based on ABA principles, that we use to teach language skills. Hart and Risley (1975) first used the strategy to increase the language skills of preschool-aged children. McGee, Daly, and Jacobs (1994) adapted the strategy for use with children who have ASDs.

When using incidental teaching, we provide instruction in the context of activities that are based on the child's interests and motivation. A major focus is on arranging the environment so children initiate language. For example, after noticing that Julie often played with puppets, Julie's teacher placed the puppets in a clear box on a shelf. The puppets were visible, but Julie could not access them without help. Julie went to the teacher, pointed and said "K." The teacher immediately looked at her and said, "Oh, you want the K puppet?" Julie said, "K puppet." The teacher gave Julie the puppet.

Using incidental teaching techniques, we can also help children expand their language. The teacher could model a longer response—"I want the K puppet"—or ask a guiding question such as "What kind of puppet?" When Julie responded, she would immediately be rewarded with the puppet that was so reinforcing to her.

The least-to-most prompting procedure described by McGee et al. (1994) provides helpful guidelines for implementing incidental teaching. After capturing or contriving a child's motivation:

- Wait for the child to self-initiate.
- Ask the generic question, "What do you need to do?"
- Say what is expected.

- Show (gesture) to indicate expectation.
- Prompt to complete interaction.

JOINT ACTION ROUTINES

Joint action routines (JARs) involve creating routines that are motivating to a child and then arranging the environment so that the child wants to initiate interaction with others.

Snyder-McLean, Solomonson, McLean, and Sack (1984) created the basic elements of JARs. Set up a routine so:

- there is joint focus due to the motivating element for the child;
- it is logical and the child can predict the outcome;
- it includes a structure for turn taking as well as an opportunity for exchanging roles;
- it is repeated enough times to provide children with the opportunity to practice the desired behavior in each role and the sequence of events to learn skills such as turn taking and waiting; and
- that once well-developed, the routine may be sabotaged to provide more opportunity for using language. Teachers can do this by:
  - » interrupting the routine or violating expectations,
  - » omitting the necessary materials,
  - » introducing new materials,
  - » initiating the routine and "playing possum,"
  - » initiating old routines with new content, and
  - » introducing new routines with old content.

For instance, Deonte loved a letter puzzle. His teacher began a session with Deonte by withholding the puzzle pieces and providing him with the correct letters as he requested them. Each time he put in a piece, his teacher said, "It fits!" Soon, Deonte started making the request, putting the puzzle piece in, and saying, "It fits." Once the routine was well established, his teacher began to give Deonte the wrong letter, giving him the opportunity to ask for the one he wanted and/or make a comment. Initially, his teacher modeled such language as, "Oops! That's the wrong one!" or "Oh! You wanted the Q!" Deonte used these expressions and some of his own, such as, "Oh no, that's not right!" and "Uh-oh, that's the wrong one!"

PEER INTERVENTIONS

Peer interventions involve other children in teaching children with ASD. First, peers may act as social models during instruction. For example, the peers may be asked questions first, so that they demonstrate good answers. Or they may be asked to take the first turn in a game to show others what is expected.

Next, peers might serve as social facilitators. In this situation, peers (rather than adults) might provide prompts for greetings, making comments, having conversations, or participating in group activities. Third, peers can actually create the learning opportunities. In this case, a peer might be coached to hold onto a toy and wait for a child to ask before providing it. Last, peers can also be assigned as buddies (Baker, 2003; Bellini, 2006). Buddies can serve several roles, including acting as conversation partners at lunch, play partners at recess, tutoring partners in class, and/or coaches during arrival and departure.

We have found it best to ask for volunteers for peer interventions, as some children are more interested in helping than others. It is particularly important that children not feel pressured or uncomfortable with their roles. Some steps for asking peers to act as models or facilitators include:

1. Identify the activity.
2. Select the behaviors that need to be modeled.
3. Determine if there are any leadership or facilitation skills needed.
4. Choose peers who are willing and able to help.
5. Provide training to the peers.

A peer training session for teaching peers to be models for Sho to take a turn would go something like this:

We're going to help Sho play a game with these fish and fishing pole. You can see that you can catch a fish by holding the hook close to the fish. *(Demonstrate that holding the magnetic "hook" near the magnetic fish allows the fish to be caught.)*

To get a fish, you'll need to request a turn to go fishing. It's your job to model asking for a turn so that Sho will know what to do.

Let's practice playing the game ourselves and then we'll play with Sho. *(Make sure everyone can request a turn.)*

Great playing! Now, it will take Sho a little longer to ask for his turn. So after you have gotten one fish, you'll need to wait for everyone to get a fish before you can ask for another.

Sometimes we'll need to be quiet and wait for Sho to ask for a turn. And when it's your turn, ask nicely, slowly, and loudly, so Sho will be able to see what you do and hear what you say.

A peer training session for teaching peers to be buddies for Eva to play on the playground could go something like this:

Thanks for volunteering to help Eva learn to play on the playground! Every day, each person will help Eva for part of the time that we're outside. Eva wants to do three things on the playground each day, so each one of you can be her buddy for one thing. Her favorite things are sliding, swinging, and crawling through the tunnel. Who wants to help Eva with sliding? Thanks, Nick! Who wants to help Eva with swinging? Great, Kari! So, Annie, are you okay with helping her with crawling through the tunnel?

Now, our goal is to give Eva just a little help. But you might need to:

o Ask her to come play by saying, "Hey Eva, let's slide!"
o Remind her at the bottom of the slide to run around and climb up again.
o Help her stay in line.
o Wait for her to ask you do to the activity with her again.

PIVOTAL RESPONSE TRAINING

Pivotal Response Training (PRT) is a naturalistic teaching strategy based on principles of ABA. This strategy, developed by Koegel and Koegel (1999), focuses on identifying and teaching pivotal skills that would directly impact a child's social and language skills. Rather than teaching many isolated skills, one at a time, PRT focuses on important behaviors that can make a big difference in many areas of language and social interaction.

The four pivotal skills are: motivation, responsivity to multiple cues, self-management, and initiations. PRT techniques for increasing motivation involve teaching in a natural setting, following the child's lead to what is interesting and desirable, varying tasks, controlling those items that a child desires, interspersing multiple teaching sessions with maintenance tasks throughout the day, and immediately reinforcing attempts.

For instance, Manny's mother noticed that he had great interest in the iPad they had just purchased. Manny reached out toward the iPad. His mother said "iPad?", waited for him to imitate her response, and then let him play with it. Later in the day, she again gained control of the iPad and repeated the process. After several days, Manny's mom repeated this process, but waited for Manny to make some approximation of the word. When he did, she immediately reinforced him with the iPad. Over time, Manny began to request the iPad from his mom independently.

Teaching children to respond to multiple cues helps them to then generalize those skills to the natural environment. Burke and Cerniglia (1990) taught children with ASD to respond to four different cues related to color (red or blue), size (big or little), type of object (pencil or crayon), and location (in the box or in the cup) of the object. With systematic instruction, children gradually learned to respond to all four cues. That is, they could correctly put "a little blue pencil in the cup" or a "big red crayon in the box." These children also improved their responses to more natural verbal instructions at school and home.

Kalli's teacher wanted her to take more responsibility for greeting her friends throughout the day. Each morning, she gave Kalli a chart with a list of five friends. She guided Kalli through the process of greeting each friend and showed her how to make a tally mark beside the friend's name. She and Kalli decided that for every morning that Kalli had all five tally marks, she could invite one of her friends to watch a video at the end of the day. Kalli quickly mastered the task of greeting friends and now uses her self-management chart to increase initiations of conversations.

Controlled Presentations

BEHAVIORAL REHEARSALS

Behavioral rehearsals are opportunities to act out behaviors and learn them so that they can become skills (Bandura, 1977). These practice opportunities should include receiving reinforcement. Role-playing is one type of behavioral rehearsal. A fun way to set up role-plays is to allow the children to become "actors" and "act" out a scenario. Even more fun for some children is to have the teacher video the role-play and watch it on a big screen. To be most effective, the role-play must involve demonstrations, instructions, prompting, and feedback. This is a good time to remember that unless meaningful reinforcement is provided, it is unlikely that the children will use the skill in the future. The games in this book often use this teaching method to help reinforce students' learning.

Schrandt, Townsend, and Poulson (2009) used behavioral rehearsals (along with other ABA techniques) with children with ASD to increase responses of empathy toward puppets who demonstrated pain, sadness, or frustration. Children rehearsed and were reinforced for such responses as "Are you okay?" and patting the puppet's arm when the puppet said "Ouch!" after bumping its leg. Responses similar to "Want some help?" and reaching to help were also recorded when the puppet said, "I broke it!" after holding up a broken LEGO™ model.

DIRECT INSTRUCTION

Siegfried Engelmann (1968) developed Direct Instruction (DI) as a scripted approach to instruction, emphasizing systematic instruction delivered at a fast pace with high levels of child engagement. Key elements of DI include presentation of small segments of a logically sequenced curriculum, frequent assessment, high rates of positive reinforcement, and clear criteria for mastery of skills.

DI programs that are thoroughly scripted are generally referred to with capital letters (DI); however, the key characteristics of this method are often used in unscripted teaching practices labeled direct instruction (di).

The features of direct instruction are:

- breaking down complex tasks into their component skills;
- providing mass practice on a specific skill until mastery is reached;
- delivering high rates of positive reinforcement;
- providing specific, immediate, corrective feedback for errors;
- eliciting frequent responses at a rapid pace;
- providing systematic review;
- interspersing new material with mastered material;
- alternating individual and group responses; and
- facilitating responding by using teacher signals.

The steps for using direct instruction (di) include the following:
- Identify a skill to be taught.
- Develop a task analysis of the skill.
- Choose the first step to teach.
- Determine the cues. (For example, the teacher points to herself while speaking and points to the children when she expects them to respond.)
- Tell and show the children what to do. (For example, say [and model] something like: "A good thing to say when you see someone walk over to the basketball court is, 'Do you want to play?'")
- Ask the children to respond to a question based on the direct instruction (e.g., "What's a good thing to say when someone comes over to the basketball court?").

DISCRETE TRIAL TRAINING

Discrete Trial Training (DTT), based on Applied Behavior Analysis, is a teaching procedure that uses clear, concise, direct instruction to teach specific skills. A discrete trial, as described by Smith (2001), is a small unit of instruction that includes a teacher's cue and prompt, a response from the child, a consequence provided by the teacher, and an intertrial break. Discrete Trial Training consists of many of these units of instruction, or trials, often taught with a most-to-least prompting hierarchy. Trials of instruction are provided on a single behavior in a massed fashion (one after another) with only a brief pause between trials.

DTT can be used to teach very basic skills such as imitation and matching as well as early language vocabulary such as labels for objects and actions. DTT is also helpful in teaching individual steps of complex tasks such as shoe tying or hand washing. In addition, vocabulary such as more and less and my and your and even skills such as predicting what is about to happen or summarizing the main idea of a paragraph can be taught with DTT.

At the beginning of instruction, there are five parts to a discrete trial. They include:

- the *discriminative stimulus* (S^D) or the prompt, cue, or other stimulus used to set the occasion for the child's response;
- a *prompt* (when needed) or the added stimulus used to ensure the child makes the correct response;
- the child's response, which can be correct (+), incorrect (-), or listed as "not responding" (NR);
- the teacher's feedback, which for a correct response should be positive; for an incorrect or no response, the teacher provides corrective information; and
- an intertrial break or a short pause to make the trials discrete (separate). It can also be an opportunity to rearrange the materials.

Once instruction is flowing, it is possible that each trial will have four parts. The prompt may not be needed during trials of mastered material. DTT that is effective moves at a fast pace and keeps the rate of success high. If a child is making errors, additional prompting is needed.

The following is an example of DTT related to social skills.

Teaching Objective: The child will be able to tell who can see an object and who cannot see the object.

Steps:
- Select a big object (such as a toy fire truck) and place it in the middle of the room.
- Determine what the stimulus will be, such as "Can Hannah see the fire truck?" This will become the first discriminative stimulus (S^D). A second, follow-up S^D could be something like, "How do you know Hannah can (can't) see the fire truck?"
- Put two chairs by the fire truck, one facing the fire truck and one facing away from the fire truck.
- Ask two children to sit in the chairs. For example, ask Hannah to sit facing the fire truck and Juan to sit facing away from the fire truck.
- Start Discrete Trial Training with dialogue such as in Figure 10.

Further Training: Some children may need multiple opportunities to practice the above skills. For example, if the child is incorrect on trial #2, repeat trial #1 (with the prompt), and then try trial #2 again. The teacher feedback for errors could be something like "Try again" or "Wait, Hannah *can* see the fire truck."

Once the child is accurate in alternating between these two children, add other children (and perhaps another object instead of the first one). This will help children generalize the skill to different people and different objects.

When the child is ready, add the follow-up S^D. The trials will look similar to those in Figure 11.

Trial #1	**Teacher (S^D): Can Hannah see the fire truck?**
	Teacher (Prompt): Yes, Hannah can see the fire truck.
	Child (Response): Yes, Hannah can see the fire truck.
	Teacher (Feedback): That's right! Hannah can see the fire truck.
	Intertrial Break (short pause of 2 to 3 seconds)
Trial #2	**Teacher (S^D): Can Hannah see the fire truck?**
	Child (Response): Yes, Hannah can see the fire truck.
	Teacher (Feedback): That's right! Hannah can see the fire truck.
	Intertrial Break (short pause of 2 to 3 seconds)
Trial #3	**Teacher (S^D): Can Juan see the fire truck?**
	Teacher (Prompt): No, Juan cannot see the fire truck.
	Child (Response): No, Juan cannot see the fire truck.
	Teacher (Feedback): That's right! Juan cannot see the fire truck.
	Intertrial Break (short pause of 2 to 3 seconds)
Trial #4	**Teacher (S^D): Can Juan see the fire truck?**
	Child (Response): No, Juan cannot see the fire truck.
	Teacher (Feedback): That's right! Juan cannot see the fire truck.
	Intertrial Break (short pause of 2 to 3 seconds)

Figure 10. Sample DTT dialogue.

The dialogues in Figures 10 and 11 are simplified for this example. When children are capable of learning the perspective of another person, they probably are able to understand and use less repetitive phrasing. However, if the child is making errors, consider using consistent phrasing such as that in Figures 10 and 11.

DISCRIMINATION TRAINING

Good direct instruction and Discrete Trial Training are composed of discrimination training. This involves teaching children to tell the differences between two or more things. Simple discriminations for social skills training might involve distinguishing between places where it is okay to yell (e.g., sports games) and places where it is not okay to yell (e.g., library). More complex discriminations might be teaching children to distinguish between effective ways to start conversations and ineffective ways to start conversations. Using controlled presentations, we would provide examples of conversation starters and conversation stoppers. For example, we might provide the following list:

Trial #1	Teacher (S^D): Can Hannah see the fire truck?
	Child (Response): Yes, Hannah can see the fire truck.
	Teacher (Feedback): That's right! Hannah can see the fire truck.
	Teacher (S^D): How do you know Hannah can see the fire truck?
	Teacher (Prompt): Her eyes are looking at it.
	Child (Response): Her eyes are looking at it.
	Teacher (Feedback): That's right! Hannah can see the fire truck because her eyes are looking at it.
	Intertrial Break
Trial #2	Teacher (S^D): Can Hannah see the fire truck?
	Child (Response): Yes, Hannah can see the fire truck.
	Teacher (Feedback): That's right! Hannah can see the fire truck.
	Teacher (S^D): How do you know Hannah can see the fire truck?
	Child (Response): Her eyes are looking at it.
	Teacher (Feedback): That's right! Hannah can see the fire truck because her eyes are looking at it.
	Intertrial Break
Trial #3	Teacher (S^D): Can Juan see the fire truck?
	Teacher (Prompt): No, Juan cannot see the fire truck.
	Child (Response): No, Juan cannot see the fire truck.
	Teacher (Feedback): That's right! Juan cannot see the fire truck.
	Teacher (S^D): How do you know Juan cannot see the fire truck?
	Teacher (Prompt): The fire truck is behind him.
	Child (Response): The fire truck is behind him.
	Teacher (Feedback): That's right! Juan cannot see the fire truck because it is behind him.
	Intertrial Break
Trial #4	Teacher (S^D): Can Juan see the fire truck?
	Child (Response): No, Juan cannot see the fire truck.
	Teacher (Feedback): That's right! Juan cannot see the fire truck.
	Teacher (S^D): How do you know Juan cannot see the fire truck?
	Child (Response): The fire truck is behind him.
	Teacher (Feedback): That's right! Juan cannot see the fire truck because it is behind him.

Figure 11. Expanded DTT dialogue.

Effective Conversation Starters	Ineffective Conversation Starters
Last night, I had pizza.	Your shirt is ugly.
What's your favorite movie?	I don't like LEGOs™.
Did you see the game last night?	I only like to talk about outer space.

Following the presentation of such examples, we then provide other examples, asking children to make a judgment about whether the statement would be an effective conversation starter or not. Then, we might ask children to brainstorm some additional examples of effective ways to start conversations.

Environmental Engineering Approaches

ACTIVITY SCHEDULES

Activity Schedules (McClannahan & Krantz, 1999) are visual supports (pictures, line drawings, symbols, or words) that represent a sequence of steps needed to complete an activity. They are designed to help build independence. Activity schedules provide children directions on what to do and information about what they will earn when they are finished.

Initially, the schedule can be housed in some type of three-ring notebook. This in itself creates a natural beginning and ending to each step of the task. On each page of the notebook, put a picture of the activity or the word on a page. On the last page, place the reinforcer that the child is rewarded with for completing the entire task. Activity schedules can also be lists like the examples in Figure 12. Pictures can also be made of separate laminated squares with Velcro™ so that they can be easily changed.

When teaching the children how to use the activity schedule, consider using most-to-least prompting. It is important to use physical prompts or gestures rather than verbal prompts, as verbal prompts are sometimes more difficult to fade. Because the goal is independence, it's best to keep the number of verbal directions at a minimum.

CARTOONING

Cartooning involves making visual representations of a conversation. These can help children with ASDs analyze interactions between or among people. For example, a teacher could provide an explanation such as this one about the cartoon in Figure 13:

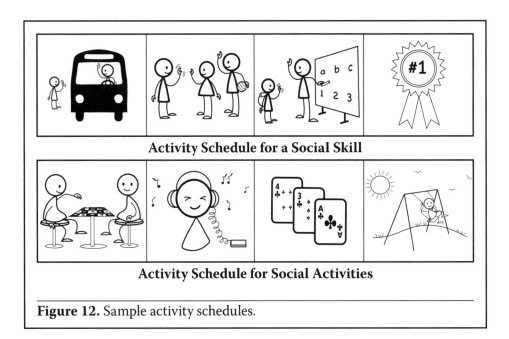

Activity Schedule for a Social Skill

Activity Schedule for Social Activities

Figure 12. Sample activity schedules.

Look at the picture I've drawn here. Remember, Jacob and Laurie were talking to each other. Then, I drew a picture of you coming up and saying, "Hey! I want to talk, too!" Now, let's look at what they might have been thinking.

The value of having a visual aid for such an explanation is that it stays there to support the discussion. In a typical discussion without visual aids, the words are gone as soon as they are said. In this case, the visual supports stay, increasing the chance that the child could make a connection between his behavior and what his friends are thinking.

Comic Strip Conversations™, developed by Carol Gray (1995), use symbols and stick drawings to represent conversations. As in standard cartoons, the characters' speech and thoughts are represented by speech bubbles and thinking balloons. Sometimes, colors are used to indicate feelings and beliefs. When teaching a child how to use cartooning or Comic Strip Conversations™, it is important to show the child how to use the speech bubbles and thought balloons. Gray (1995) suggested using "small talk" with an adult to formulate the conversation. The adult asks the child guiding questions such as "Who was there?" and "What did you do?"

COMMUNICATION TEMPTATIONS

Communication temptations (Wetherby & Prizant, 1989) are contrived or engineered situations that entice children to use language. Examples include eating a desired food item in front of the child without offering any to the child;

Figure 13. Sample cartoon.

activating a wind-up toy, letting it deactivate, and handing it to the child; playing a familiar social game with the child until the child expresses pleasure, then stopping the game and waiting; and opening a jar of bubbles, then closing the jar tightly, and handing the closed jar to the child.

To use communication temptations, set up the communication temptation and then model the language you want the child to use. A good model will be slightly more advanced than what the child can do independently. Use shaping procedures to reward attempts at communication, gradually expecting better and more refined language.

INCREDIBLE 5-POINT SCALE

The Incredible 5-Point Scale (Buron & Curtis, 2008) helps children manage their emotions and behavior through the use of visual scales. Children first learn to describe their own actions and physiology and label their thinking and feelings (such as anger, fear, or pain, and the stage of the emotion) and then identify techniques to move up or down on the scale. For example, to represent anger at the top of an intensity scale, we coached Lance to describe his actions (such as clinching fists and screaming) and his physiology (such as tense muscles and fast breathing). Then, we guided Lance to describe his thinking (e.g., "It's not perfect" or "I can't get anything right") and his feelings (e.g., "I'm so mad!" or "I'm filled with anger!") Once the scale was developed, we taught Lance a relaxation procedure to help him learn to move his actions to a lower level on the scale. Once he was relaxed and back in a stage of reasonable thinking, we provided discussions to challenge such irrational thoughts as "I should be able to make everything perfect" or "I can't make mistakes." Working to shape his thinking, we reinforced statements such as "It's not possible to do perfect work all the time" and "Everybody makes mistakes." Lance also worked collaboratively with his behavior consultant to write and review a Social Story™ called "Everyone Makes Mistakes." The Social Story™ included his version of the 5-Point Scale to help provide a visual support of the stages of his anger.

Steps for using the 5-Point Scale include:

- Choose a target behavior such as laughing appropriately at jokes.
- Create the scale, using behavioral language to describe each level of the scale (see Figure 14).
- Develop strategies to teach the child to use the scale to recognize the behaviors on each level of the scale. This might include watching demonstrations of the behaviors at each level and/or watching videos of the behaviors at each level of the scale.
- Help the child practice adjusting his or her behavior, keeping as closely to the target behavior as possible. This might include reading a Social Story™, participating in behavioral rehearsals, or practicing calming procedures.

POWER CARDS

Power cards outline a brief situation or scenario related to a challenging behavior or behavior problem. They can be small cards that can be laminated and carried in a pocket, wallet, or purse. They can also be taped inside a notebook or assignment pad.

Power cards are developed around a special interest of the child with ASDs. Common power cards are designed around movie or music stars, famous athletes, action figures, or superheroes. The card reminds children that the person of special interest would be proud of them for demonstrating appropriate or acceptable behavior. See Figure 15 for an example of a power card.

PRIMING

Children with autism may experience anxiety or stress related to anticipating upcoming activities or events. It may be helpful to review expectations, rules, and materials prior to the event. Priming is an intervention that helps prepare children ahead of time for situations that may be challenging. The purpose of priming is to increase the child's familiarity with expectations and materials, provide predictability, and increase the possibility of success. Priming is a simple strategy that takes a short amount of time, usually 10 minutes or less, yet goes a long way for promoting success for the child.

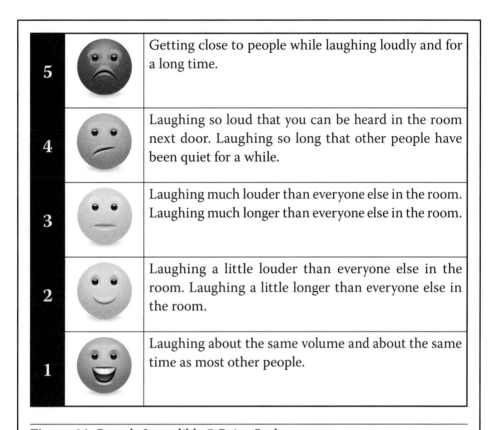

5		Getting close to people while laughing loudly and for a long time.
4		Laughing so loud that you can be heard in the room next door. Laughing so long that other people have been quiet for a while.
3		Laughing much louder than everyone else in the room. Laughing much longer than everyone else in the room.
2		Laughing a little louder than everyone else in the room. Laughing a little longer than everyone else in the room.
1		Laughing about the same volume and about the same time as most other people.

Figure 14. Sample Incredible 5-Point Scale.

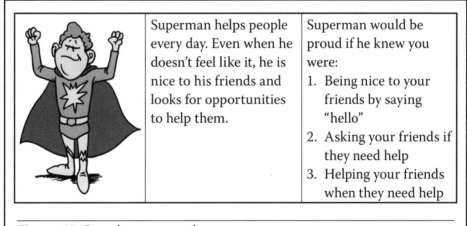

	Superman helps people every day. Even when he doesn't feel like it, he is nice to his friends and looks for opportunities to help them.	Superman would be proud if he knew you were:
		1. Being nice to your friends by saying "hello"
		2. Asking your friends if they need help
		3. Helping your friends when they need help

Figure 15. Sample power card.

During the first few weeks of recess on the playground, Jamie would throw dirt, push other children, and smile as the other children ran away. Jamie's teacher made a visual prompt to show him what he "can" and "cannot" do on the playground. He was shown pictures of "can throw a ball back and forth with a friend," "cannot throw dirt," "can say 'go' to a friend," and "cannot push a friend." Each day before recess, Jamie's teacher primed him by showing him the visual prompt and verbally reminding him of the rules. Jamie was able to engage in acceptable behavior such as tossing the ball back and forth with peers and saying "go" to initiate a game of chase with his friends.

SENSORY INTERVENTIONS

From a behavioral perspective, we find information related to sensory intervention useful for two purposes. First, it helps us make hypotheses about functions of behavior. In other words, we can gain an understanding of a possible reason for the behavior. For example, observing that Katie covers her ears and resists entering the cafeteria encourages us to hypothesize that she is avoiding the noise in the cafeteria. Of course, once we verify the function of the behavior, then we can provide a more effective intervention for it.

Second, information from sensory interventions is useful for using sensory activities as antecedents and consequences that can increase or decrease the chance that a target behavior will occur. In our experience, children who seem to lack energy often benefit from sensory activities that increase alertness. Other children are very hyperactive and need sensory activities that help use up some energy and slow them down in order to focus. Also, sensory activities can be highly reinforcing and can often be powerful incentives for rewarding socially appropriate behavior.

Research is still mixed on the efficacy of sensory interventions; however, there are a number of positive studies (Miller, Schoen, Coll, Brett-Green, & Reale, 2005) and a great deal of anecdotal support for the technique. Research does clearly show that children with ASD can be oversensitive (hyper) or undersensitive (hypo) to stimuli in the environment. Baranek (2002) summarized 29 studies and information from 757 individuals regarding the sensory and motor difficulties seen in individuals with ASD. With regard to treatment that includes sensory interventions, Baranek suggested a conservative approach supervised by trained professionals using accepted data collection and evaluation methods.

There are seven sensory systems (vestibular, proprioceptive, visual, auditory, gustatory, olfactory, and tactile) that might be affected in children with ASD. Many occupational therapists are trained to evaluate the sensory needs of children with ASD and to make recommendations for school personnel and parents to implement. Recommendations for the vestibular or proprioceptive systems include weighted vests, seat cushions, and gross motor exercises such as bouncing, swinging, and spinning. Sometimes, children with ASD do well with sunglasses or visors for visual accommodations, earplugs or headphones for auditory accommodations, crunchy foods or blowing bubbles for gustatory accommodations, scented stickers or nose plugs for olfactory accommodations, and weighted vests or protective gloves for tactile accommodations.

SOCIAL SCRIPT INTERVENTIONS

Social scripts and script fading procedures are designed to teach children with ASD the art of conversation (Krantz & McClannahan, 1998). Scripts are written words, phrases, or sentences that a child is taught to say in order to participate in a conversation. When prompts are needed for children to participate in conversations, these written scripts replace an adult's verbal prompts. Similar to scripts that actors use to learn to play their parts, social scripts help children with ASD learn what to say when talking with others.

Scripts may be effective because, as visual supports, they remain in place as long as the child needs them. A verbal prompt or direction is gone as soon as it is said, but the visual prompt remains in place until the child can participate in conversations without them. Scripts can help the child see the whole exchange of a conversation without the potentially confusing verbal interruptions of an adult.

Scripts are developed based on the individual language level and preferences of children as well as their interests, favorite topics, and any special talents. As a simple conversation example, Jonathan and Jason were seated across a table, each with a stack of cards. The cards included questions and answers such as:

Jonathan: I brought a peanut butter sandwich for lunch. What did you bring?
Jason: I brought pizza. What do you have to drink?
Jonathan: I have chocolate milk. How about you?

When teaching a child how to use the script, it is always helpful to have a prompter along with a conversation partner. The prompter helps the child by orienting him toward the conversation partner, pointing to the script, and waiting for the child to read. As the child progresses, the prompter fades the prompts until the child can follow the process independently. Once the child uses the script to communicate, fade the script by omitting the last word, and then the last two words, and so forth. For instance, if the original script says, "I like pizza," it is then faded to "I like," and then just "I."

After being presented with many scripts, children often use the language from the scripts in other conversations, combine scripts with language modeled by their conversation partners, and/or generate language independently from past conversations. Scripts can help children have conversations with their peers, parents, siblings, and teachers about many of their activities and interests.

For children who can't read, audio cards can be used as scripts. Using most-to-least prompting, the children are taught to run a prerecorded card through a card reader (or recorder, iPod, or iPad), listen, and then imitate the word, phrase, or sentence. In some cases, pictures and symbols can be used to make the script. In any case, the procedure is similar in that scripts are used as prompts to help the child expand the language used to converse with a partner. When possible, the scripts are faded gradually and systematically.

SOCIAL STORIES™

A Social Story™ is a short story that describes a situation, concept, or social skill using a format that is meaningful for children. The story needs a title, a clear introduction, a body describing the situation, and a conclusion emphasizing the most important concepts of the story (Gray, 2010). Gray (1995) described the purpose of the Social Story™ as providing the child with a greater understanding of the social situation or skill, not specifically to change the child's behavior.

Writing a Social Story™ involves identifying and analyzing a situation that is challenging for the child. For instance, every time Terry entered the cafeteria for lunch, he walked on his tiptoes and flapped his hands. His teacher first suspected that the cafeteria environment was too loud. However, because Terry seemed relaxed in the loud gym, she investigated the lunch routine at his previous school. There, the children ate in a small room and the adults served them. The routine at the new school involved going to the cafeteria, standing in line, and buying milk. Suspecting that Terry was reacting to this change of routine, his teachers developed a Social Story™ called Buying Milk at School.

To help write effective Social Stories™, Gray (2010) suggested using these sentences:

- *Descriptive sentences* are statements that explain facts about the situation such as where a situation occurs, who is involved, and what they are doing. Each story should have more descriptive sentences than any other type of sentence. For example, in Terry's story, the descriptive sentences included: "At this school most children eat lunch in the cafeteria. Children who want milk buy it in the cafeteria. To buy milk, children walk through the line, choose the kind they like, and pay the cashier."
- *Perspective sentences* describe opinions or feelings about the situation. Most of the time, perspective sentences refer to the opinions or feelings of other people. For example, "Some children think it's fun to choose the kind of milk that they want to drink. Many adults in the cafeteria like to help children get their milk and walk through the line."

- *Affirmative sentences* describe a commonly shared point of view and add a value statement to emphasize the importance of the social skills described. For example, "Sometimes going through the line and getting milk is new for some children. That's okay. There are adults and friends to help children get their milk in the cafeteria."
- *Coaching sentences* describe who will be involved and what they will do to help the child succeed. They may describe choices the child might make or self-management strategies. For example, "The adults in the cafeteria will walk around and ask children if they need help. When I want to buy milk I will try to get in line, choose the milk I want and pay the cashier."
- *Partial sentences* allow the child to participate, take ownership of the story, and review critical concepts. These statements are written in a fill-in-the-blank format, so a part of a sentence is replaced with a blank space. After the child has reviewed the story a few times, any of the types of sentences described above can be used as a partial sentence. For example, "When I want to buy milk at school, I can try to _____."

Once the story is created, make plans to introduce the story, review it with the child, and then adapt the story, if needed, based on the child's response. It is important to follow the child's lead, use the story as necessary, and fade the story as the child progresses.

STRUCTURED TEACHING

Structured Teaching, a part of the TEACCH (Treatment and Education of Autistic and Related Communication-Handicapped Children) approach, is a program designed around understanding and accommodating the needs of children with autism. With the goal of increasing independence, the environment is modified to make clear what the children are expected to do. There are four main components of the TEACCH approach (Schopler, Mesibov, & Hearsey, 1995):

- *Physical organization* refers to the modifications of the physical layout of the classroom and work areas. For example, Emily's classroom is designed so that she sits next to a volunteer peer buddy. Her desk has a workspace designated by a rectangle of green tape and she has a box of materials fixed to the upper left corner of her desk with Velcro™. Her teacher has a basket in the front of the room labeled "Finished Work." Emily also has a line of tape on the floor near the door, helping her find her place to stand when the class lines up to leave the room.
- *Schedules* reduce anxiety and frustration by letting children know what activities will take place and in what sequence (Schopler et al., 1995). They assist children in organizing themselves, remembering what to do,

and predicting events. For example, Kerry's visual schedule (see Figure 16) is a list of his activities for the day. Because he is extremely anxious about school, his day starts with a 15-minute period in the sensory room. Sometimes, Kerry needs a task broken down into steps for him. Figure 17 shares two visual schedules, one for an academic task and one for a social skill.

- *Work systems:* Work systems (Schopler et al., 1995) are visual representations designed to answer four questions to help children work independently: (a) "What should I do?", (b) "How much should I do?", (c) "How will I know if I'm finished?", and (d) "What happens next?" For example, Missy's work system is made out of a stack of paper trays numbered 1–4 from top to bottom. Her first project is always in the top paper tray. It is usually an easy, enjoyable task such as coloring a picture according to numbers. The second and third trays hold more complex worksheets reinforcing concepts she has learned in class. The last tray holds a note (such as "computer time" or "sensory activities") that describes what she has earned for completing her work. Missy works at her desk and the work system (stack of paper trays) is placed on a table to her left. A basket for finished projects is place on a table to her right.

- *Task organization* (Schopler et al., 1995) is similar to work systems in that it also helps children to complete work independently. The task is organized to help the child work systematically from top to bottom or left to right. For example, in the work system above, the task is organized for Missy to start with whatever is in the top paper tray. She works systematically from top to bottom. Other work systems might be arranged with manipulatives. For example, three activities (perhaps a puzzle, ring stand, and shape sorter) can be arranged in a line on a table. The child would be taught to work from left to right, first putting all the puzzle pieces in the frame, next putting all the rings on the stand, and last putting all the shapes in the shape box. A task system such as this might even have a reward (e.g., snack or iPad) placed to the right so that the child can access the reward independently. In a task such as this, it is often helpful to use Velcro™ to reduce the number of things that may fall off or cover up other important parts of the task. For instance, the puzzle frame, ring stand base, and shape box might be secured to the table with Velcro™. Another example of task organization involves putting out pictorial instructions and a product sample. For example, pictures of the process of assembling a flashlight and an assembled flashlight could be placed above the work area that contains the disassembled flashlight bodies, batteries, and lights.

Activity	Location	Stars!
Sensory Fun!	Sensory Room, Room 118	⭐
Early Bird Work	Second Grade, Room 224	⭐
Reading	Second Grade, Room 224	⭐
Lunch	Cafeteria	
Recess	Outside or in Room 224	
Math	Second Grade, Room 224	
Science/Social Studies	Learning Lab, Room 345	
Announcements	Homeroom	
Line Up for Bus	Blue Hallway	

Figure 16. Visual schedule for Kerry.

VIDEO MODELING

Video modeling is an effective tool for assisting children in developing a wide range of social skills (Charlop-Christy & Daneshvar, 2003). The model can be a peer (peer modeling) or the child (self-modeling). The most effective peer modeling, as demonstrated by Bandura (1977), involves a model peer who approximates the characteristics of the child who will be imitating the model. We have found that video self-modeling (VSM) is especially effective, perhaps because children enjoy watching themselves on screen.

Today's Reading	Done!	Greeting Friends	Did it!
Read Section 1 to your partner.	✓	Walk up to a friend, but stay an arm's length away	✚
Tell your partner what happened in Section 1.	✓	Say, "Hi, Brian," or "Hi, Michael!"	✚
Listen to your partner read Section 2.	✓	Wait for your friend to say "Hi."	✚
Ask your partner "What happened in Section 2?"	✓	Say, "What's up?" "What's new?" or "What's happening?"	✚
Read Section 3 to your partner.		Wait for your partner to answer and listen for a question.	✚
Tell your partner what happened in Section 3.		Either answer the question or say a little something.	
Draw a picture of what happened in the story.		Listen for a response and make a comment about what your friend said.	
Answer your teacher's questions about the story.		When the conversation is over, say something like, "Nice talking to you!"	

Figure 17. Two broken-down visual schedules.

Saunders and Lo (2011) described multiple steps for implementing video modeling. To begin the process, first decide on the targeted skill. For example, Jerry has been sitting too close to his peers in small group work. The targeted skill was determined to be sitting at least an arm's length away from his peers. Next, decide on a video area that is free of extraneous stimuli and develop a script that is reviewed with the model. Then, make a video that is about 3 to 5 minutes long and review it with the child.

In Jerry's video, Mike (the peer model), approached a group of boys sitting in a science lab. As he walked, he said, "I am going to sit at least an arm's length away from my friends." He then sat down, carefully looking to check his distance. In the next scene, he approached and sat with a group of peers in homeroom, and in the last scene, he approached and sat with a group of peers at lunch.

Jerry watched the videos with his teacher, reviewed the rule, and commented on how it was followed. Jerry watched the videos three times a week for 2 weeks; after doing so, his memory for sitting an arm's length away was excellent.

Video self-modeling consists of making videos such as the one above, but using the target child as the model in the video. Buggey (2005) described the process as one that allows children to see themselves performing above their current level. For example, Eli was not safe in crossing the street himself and vigorously resisted holding the hand of an adult while crossing the street. His teachers made a video called "Crossing the Street With Eli," which starred Eli crossing the street carefully while holding an adult's hand. The video site selected was a part of the school driveway that looked like a street. While one teacher taped, another teacher held Eli's hand, walked him slowly to the curb, and told him to take a long look in each direction. Eli was rewarded with a small candy each time he followed the instructions. With editing, the teacher's instructions were eliminated and all scenes that involved Eli dashing across the street were cut. The final video was pieced together and a voice-over described the steps for crossing the street. Of course, music, titles (such as "Starring Eli!"), and clapping were inserted to make the video fun to watch. Eli watched the video often and, in the future, willingly held the hand of an adult while crossing the street.

VISUAL SUPPORTS

There are many kinds of visual supports that can help children with social skills. Here, we have provided descriptions and examples of visual schedules, cue cards, people locators, checklists, graphic organizers, and consequence maps. These visual supports can help:

- decrease anxiety by helping children understand and remember a sequence of events and upcoming activities,
- decrease frustration by presenting complex tasks into steps of just-manageable difficulty,
- increase motivation by helping children see their forthcoming preferred activities and/or rewards, and
- increase children's understanding of the relationship between their actions and the consequences.

Visual schedules can be created for part of a day or a full day. They can be objects, photographs, line drawings, symbols, words, or combinations. Several previous figures have shown visual schedules. Cue cards provide reminders of what to do or not do (see Figure 18). People locators (see Figure 19) provide a visual representation of where people are. Names can be made on cards and laminated. A piece of Velcro™ on the back of the name cards makes it easy to move people around to their current locations. Checklists (see Figure 20) present

✓ DO	✗ DON'T
Walk up to your friend	Walk by without talking
Stay about 3 feet away	Put your face close
Say "hi" or "hello"	Giggle

Figure 18. Sample cue card.

At School	At Home	At Work

Me	Mom	Dad
Chrissie		
Henry		

Figure 19. People locator.

Checklist for Going to a Birthday Party

_____ Ring the doorbell
_____ Say "Hi" to Miss Pat (Trevor's mom)
_____ Say "Happy Birthday" to Trevor
_____ Say "Bye" to Mom when she leaves
_____ Watch Trevor open his presents
_____ Follow directions while playing games
_____ Eat cake and ice cream
_____ Ask Trevor's mom for help if you need it
_____ Say "Hi" to Mom when she comes
_____ Say "Thank you" to Trevor and his mom when you leave

Figure 20. Sample checklist.

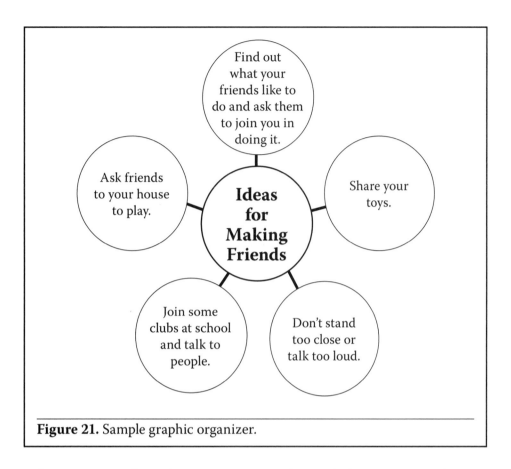

Figure 21. Sample graphic organizer.

information visually and can support or replace verbal instructions. They are particularly useful when there are multiple steps to a task or routine.

Graphic organizers (see Figure 21) are visual representations that help children brainstorm their ideas and organize their thoughts. They are often used for academic tasks, but can be very useful in teaching social skills. Here is a sample for helping children think of ideas for making friends. Another graphic organizer that is useful is a T-chart. Figure 22 is an example of how it might be used to explain specifically what behaviors look like and sound like.

Consequence maps are visual representations that show children the connections between their actions and the consequences that may or will follow. They can be designed with sentences, words, symbols, line drawings, photographs, or objects. Generally, the item on the left represents a situation or an antecedent that triggers the possibility of several behaviors. Items to the right represent various actions and their consequences. Using the example in Figure 23, Ledarious was able to see that the best way to get his friends to share was to ask them to play with him. Prior to that, Ledarious grabbed the ball, expecting his friends to chase him.

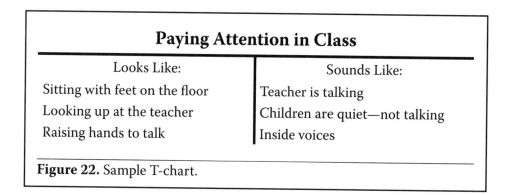

Paying Attention in Class

Looks Like:	Sounds Like:
Sitting with feet on the floor	Teacher is talking
Looking up at the teacher	Children are quiet—not talking
Raising hands to talk	Inside voices

Figure 22. Sample T-chart.

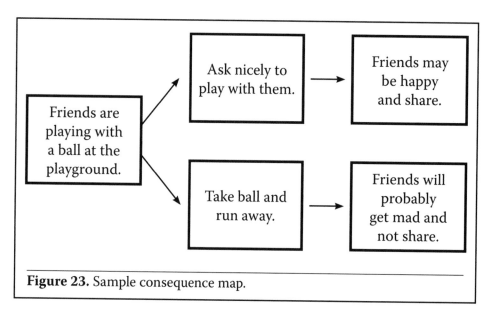

Figure 23. Sample consequence map.

Cognitive Interventions

Cognitive Behavior Modification (CBM) is based on the idea that how we think (cognition), how we feel (emotion), and how we act (behavior) all affect each other and interact together. Using CBM techniques, we can teach children to manage their behavior by developing an awareness of their feelings and engaging in rational thinking. These interventions rely on the assumption that individuals have the ability and desire to learn to monitor and manage their own behavior (Heflin & Simpson, 1998).

The following characteristics of CBM are adapted from the work of Kaplan and Carter (1995):

- Children themselves (rather than other people or events) are the primary agents for changing their own behavior.
- Models are used to help children learn thinking processes.

- Children learn to verbalize their thinking aloud and later to themselves.
- Children learn a problem-solving sequence and follow the steps to solve problems.
- Children learn self-management techniques and monitor their own behavior.

We can use CBM techniques to teach children, for example, to discover their own triggers for anxiety and, with support, develop their own ways of managing their emotions.

The example in Figure 24 is based on the steps that Quinn, Swaggart, and Myles (1994) outlined for using CBM. In this example, the target behavior is imitating others.

RELAXATION TRAINING

Relaxation Training is a process for teaching children to calm themselves down in times of high emotion or high activity. It's useful for times when children are upset and anxious as well as when they are very excited or really angry. In addition, it can be helpful when children are overexcited or hyperactive.

When you have a child who frequently gets anxious or upset, teach him routines that will help him learn to relax, such as the following:
- Take three deep breaths.
- Count to 10 slowly.
- Check to see if your muscles are relaxed. (Relaxed muscles are loose and floppy, not hard and tight.)

You can also teach routines that will help the child release stress, such as the following:
- Jump 10 times.
- Bounce a ball 10 times.
- Check to see if you can talk in a quiet voice. (A quiet voice cannot be heard on the other side of the room.)

It's also helpful to teach children preventative measures for keeping calm in situations when they might get frustrated. Children can:
- use a visual schedule to predict upcoming events,
- ask for a break to go to a preapproved "chill-out" room or other safe place, or
- change to another task that is less frustrating or anxiety producing.

Step 1: Model—The teacher says something like:

When I walk into the classroom, I look around at everyone else in the room. Because they are sitting down, I'll sit down, too. Now, I'm noticing that they all have books out to read. I'm getting out my book to read as well.

When my friends start to put their books away, I'll put mine away, too. When I go to the playground, if everyone is playing, I'll play as well. But when I see everyone start to get in line, I'll find my place in line.

Step 2: Put-Through—The teacher says something like:

Let's go down to the gym and see what everyone is doing. Let's see if you can go in and do what they are doing. Practice put-through procedures until the child imitates class peers with minimal prompting.

Step 3: Self-Recording—The teacher says something like:

When the timer in your pocket buzzes, look around to see if you are doing what everyone else is doing. If you are, circle the word yes on your chart. If you are not, circle the word no. If you circled the word yes, whisper to yourself, "Good watching!" If not, remind yourself to watch what your peers are doing.

Figure 24. Sample CBM procedures.

SELF-MANAGEMENT STRATEGIES

Self-management strategies involve the personal application of behavior change procedures to alter our own behavior. When teaching children to use these strategies, they participate in choosing personal goals, selecting and implementing intervention procedures, and in monitoring their own progress (Cooper, Heron, & Heward, 2007).

Koegel, Singh, and Koegel (2010) have taught children with autism to self-manage their social conversations in order to promote independent interactions, which can lead to developing friendships. Children are taught the following sequence for self-managing social conversations:

1. Bring up a topic.
2. Add a little more information.
3. Ask a question.

Alexis has difficulty initiating conversations during lunch with her peers. Alexis was taught the three-step sequence listed above through role-plays. She mastered the sequence with adults and peers and is now able to initiate conversations at lunch with only a small visual representation of the sequence. For example, she will initiate with a peer by stating, "I had a fun weekend. I saw the movie *Brave*." Then she will ask a question such as, "What movies have you seen lately?" With a self-management chart, Alexis can complete this sequence at least three times during the lunch period.

SOCIAL THINKING

Winner and Crooke (2009) described Social Thinking® as a "way to train your brain to help you figure out the people around you" (p. xiv). Winner (2002) noted that she believes that when children with ASD are taught the reason for social behaviors, they are more likely to generalize those behaviors across a variety of settings.

Successful social interaction requires effective social cognition. An important aspect of understanding social interaction is determining what behaviors are expected in what environments. Instead of teaching children that their behaviors are either appropriate or inappropriate, or good or bad, she explains that it's good to think about whether behaviors are expected or unexpected in certain situations. Actions that are expected are things like sitting quietly in a restaurant or asking permission to touch things that belong to other people. Unexpected behaviors are the opposite, such as yelling out in a restaurant or picking up things that belong to someone else.

The premise of Social Thinking® is that it is important to teach children with ASD that their actions affect the thinking and feelings of others. They need to understand that people feel uncomfortable about actions that are unexpected. Because people like to feel comfortable, they avoid people who engage in actions that make them feel uncomfortable.

Baron-Cohen (1989) used the terms *mindblindness* and *Theory of Mind deficits* to describe the difficulties that children with ASD have with understanding the perspectives of others, predicting the behavior of others, and making sense of emotions. The Social Thinking® approach uses visual supports to help explain typical thinking patterns of others. For example, it is sometimes difficult for children with ASD to understand that people might be thinking things that are different from what they are saying. To explain this concept using Social Thinking strategies, a teacher might draw pictures of people talking using speech bubbles. Thought balloons are often used to represent what other people are thinking. For example, a picture could be drawn to show a person saying one thing while thinking another.

Winner and Crooke (2009) explained that the Social Thinking® strategy involves teaching perspective taking in four steps. For example, to help Jack figure out the social rules of a birthday party, provide coaching with questions such as the following.

- *Step 1: Think about the people near you.* Present the situation to students: "Tomorrow is Robby's birthday party. Let's think about ways that might help you feel comfortable and fit in at the party. This might help you relax at the party. If you're more relaxed, people might have good thoughts about you." Pose questions such as the following (potential answers are included after each question):
  - » Who will be there? (Robby, Robby's friends, and Robby's parents)
  - » Who are some of Robby's friends? (Well, he knows Alex, James, and Paul.)
  - » How will Robby's friends be feeling? (They should be happy because it's a party.)

- *Step 2: Think about why the person is near you.* Questions might include:
  - » Why are Robby's friends at the party? (To have fun, eat cake, and watch Robby open his presents.)
  - » Why might Robby's friends be near you? (They might also be trying to see him open his presents. They might be getting cake and ice cream for themselves.)

- *Step 3: Think about what other people may be thinking about you.* Questions might include:
  - » What might Robby and his friends be thinking about you? (If I wait my turn for cake and ice cream, they'll have good thoughts about me. If I break in line, they might think I'm rude.)
  - » What else might they think? (If I play the game, they might think I'm having a good time. If I yell and scream if I lose a game, they might have thoughts about me being odd or different.)

- *Step 4: Monitor and modify your own behavior.* Questions might include:
  - » What might you do at the party to stay relaxed and calm? (Wait in line and remember that no one is there to grab my cake and ice cream.)
  - » What else? (Remember that I don't have to win all the time. Games are just for fun. I'll try to stay calm when I lose and people might think I'm fun.)

SOCIAL SKILL AUTOPSIES

Lavoie (1994) developed the Social Skill Autopsy strategy to help children understand their social mistakes. This strategy involves working with children after a social error has been made. Working with an adult, children identify the mistake, assess who was affected by the mistake, and decide how to correct the mistake. The children then make a plan to practice so that the mistake is not repeated.

SODA

Another example of a cognitive intervention is the SODA strategy, developed by Bock (2001). The four steps of the strategy teach children to Stop, Observe, Deliberate, and Act (SODA). Questions in each step guide or cue the children to think through the social situation.

The questions for the first step, "Stop," help the children survey the environment and determine the room arrangement, sequence of events, or social routines associated with the setting. Questions for the second step, "Observe," prompt the child to notice what people are doing and saying in that setting. The questions for the third step, "Deliberate," assist the children to think about how other people might respond to them. Here, the children need to be able think about possible facial expressions and body language that might give them clues about how others are thinking about them. Questions for the last step, "Act," encourage children to take action based upon the results of their answers in the previous steps. Most often, the SODA strategy appears to be when children are considering the best way to initiate and maintain conversations, but we feel that it is appropriate in many additional social situations.

CHAPTER 4

Assessing and
Monitoring Social Skills

Assessing the social skill challenges of children with ASDs can be overwhelming. With so many checklists, assessments, books, and other materials available, it can be very difficult to know where to start.

We recommend that each child be assessed routinely with a complete assessment such as Assessment of Basic Language and Learning Skills (ABLLS®-R) or the Verbal Behavior Milestones Assessment and Placement Program (VB-MAPP). For more information about the ABLLS®-R, see Partington (2006a, 2006b), and for information about the VB-MAPP, see Sundberg (2008). In addition to providing a clear picture of the child's language, social, and other skills, both of these assessments serve as curriculum guides and skill tracking systems.

In this book, we have selected 10 skills to be used as examples for using the framework for teaching social skills that we describe in Chapter 4. In order to begin instruction with our framework, we have developed a brief, easy-to-use assessment targeting the 10 social skills across six skill levels. This quick checklist can serve as a guide for systematic instruction and as a tool for monitoring progress.

This is only a portion of a complete program for a child. Although we provide this checklist for a quick assessment and skill tracking charts, in no way do we wish to undermine the importance of an ongoing full and complete assessment plan.

1	The child never uses this skill.	(0 of every 5 opportunities)
2	The child occasionally uses this skill.	(1 of every 5 opportunities)
3	The child sometimes uses this skill.	(2 or 3 of every 5 opportunities)
4	The child usually uses this skill.	(4 of every 5 opportunities)
5	The child always uses this skill.	(5 of every 5 opportunities)

Figure 25. Social skills rating scale.

For the sample skills in this book, we will present a framework that helps us:

- Target a particular skill and assess that skill on a scale from 1–5.
- Use effective strategies to teach the skill at each of six levels of competence:
  - » starting with children using the skill in a fun and engaging game,
  - » continuing with children labeling the skill and saying when to use it,
  - » arranging for children to demonstrate the skill in contrived situations,
  - » providing opportunities to use the skill in the natural environment,
  - » promoting the development of higher level thinking skills, and
  - » concluding with opportunities to engage in problem solving related to the skill.

Use the guidelines in the rating scale in Figure 25 to help assess the children's current level of mastery of the social skill. Rate each skill from 1 to 5 according to the chart. Then, implement the teaching procedures and use the rating scale periodically to check the children's progress.

Now you can move on to using the checklist to assess social skills as you teach the children the activities presented in this book (see Figure 26). Figure 27 allows you to collect data on the children and track their progress on the various steps of the framework. Unless the skill is completely mastered (level 5), we recommend starting instruction at Step 1 of the framework.

Skill	Description	Rating from 1–5				
Asking Politely (Lotto)	Uses polite phrases to make requests for wants and needs	1	2	3	4	5
Responding to Directions From Friends (Simon Says)	Follows directions from other children	1	2	3	4	5
Looking Where Others Are Looking (I Spy)	Follows gaze of speaker in joint activities	1	2	3	4	5
Asking Questions (Twenty Questions)	Asks appropriate questions of adults and peers	1	2	3	4	5
Sharing Things With Others (Give Away Lotto)	Offers items to others and takes turns	1	2	3	4	5
Making Appropriate Comments During Competitive Activities (Rock, Paper, Scissors)	Uses acceptable statements for both winning and losing	1	2	3	4	5
Helping Others (Freeze Tag)	Gives and receives assistance from others	1	2	3	4	5
Asking for Permission and Accepting "No" as an Answer (Captain, May I?)	Requests permission and accepts or tolerates "no" as an answer	1	2	3	4	5
Talking With Others (Getting to Know You Bingo)	Approaches others, waits for a response, asks questions, responds to questions, and converses with others	1	2	3	4	5
Pretending With Others (Paper Bag Skits)	Takes on a role in order to engage in pretend play with others	1	2	3	4	5

Figure 26. Checklist for skills used in the games in this book.

	PLAY The child can demonstrate the skill in a game.	TALK The child can name the skill and, given a question or hypothetical situation, can say when it should be used.	ACT The child can act out the skill in a contrived or role-playing situation.	USE The child can use the skill in a natural setting.	EXPLAIN The child can explain why the skill is effective in interacting with others.	ADJUST The child can list and demonstrate alternative actions when the social skill is not effective.
Asking Politely Uses polite phrases to make requests for wants and needs						
Responding to Directions From Friends Follows directions from other children						
Looking Where Others Are Looking Follows gaze of speaker in joint activities and follows comments						
Asking Questions Asks appropriate questions of adults and peers						
Sharing Things With Others Gives items to others and takes turns						

Figure 27. Data collection chart.

	PLAY	TALK	ACT	USE	EXPLAIN	ADJUST
Making Appropriate Comments During Competitive Activities Uses acceptable statements for both winning and losing						
Helping Others Gives and receives assistance from others						
Asking for Permission and Accepting "No" as an Answer Requests permission and accepts or tolerates "no" as an answer						
Talking With Others Approaches others, waits for a response, asks questions, responds to questions, and converses with others						
Pretending With Others Takes on a role in order to engage in pretend play with others						

Figure 27. Continued

CHAPTER 5

Using the Complete the Puzzle Framework

When teaching social skills to children with ASDs, it is important to understand that problems with social skills can occur for several reasons. First, it's possible that the child does not know what to do. Second, it's possible that the child knows what to do, but can't get started. Third, it's possible that the child attempted to use the social skill and experienced a lack of success. Fourth, it's possible that the child knows what to do and chooses not to do it.

In the case of children with ASDs, our experience has taught us that the majority of children lack social skills for the first three reasons. That makes it important to do a thorough job of teaching. We can't just tell the child what to do. We must teach it with thoughtful, systematic instruction. In our opinion, this includes providing many opportunities to practice the skill, name the skill, use the skill in many settings with many people, explain the skill, and adjust the skill when it's not working.

The Complete the Puzzle framework we use in this book is divided into six steps for developing competence in each social skill. Each step is defined by an objective and the steps increase in difficulty, beginning with an easy and fun way to practice the skill and ending with opportunities to use flexible thinking when using the skill with others. Carefully planned instruction is required and progress is documented as children earn puzzle pieces for their success at each step. When all six puzzle pieces are earned, we consider that child to have "completed the puzzle" for that social skill.

The framework can easily be adapted for early learners, intermediate learners, and advanced learners. Early learners are those who have developed very few social skills and may still need intensive instruction on basic language skills. They are able to learn to interact with others, but, at least at this point, are most likely to learn social skills as rules or procedures. They are in the process of developing basic skills such as imitating, making requests, and following one-word directions. They may need many hours of intensive instruction to learn to make polite requests, wait for a turn, share highly prized items, or learn from observing others. Many of these children do not appear to value interaction with their peers.

Intermediate learners are those who have developed basic social skills such as making polite requests of others, following directions composed of several words or steps, waiting to take a turn, and sharing with others. They have learned some skills by watching others, but still require significant assistance to interact effectively with others. Most of these children interact with peers by following rules and procedures and, with good instruction, are able to learn to adjust their behavior to different social situations. However, most children will encounter significant challenges in developing the abstract concepts and abilities to understand the perspective of others required for social thinking.

Advanced learners are those who have learned many socials skills, but are still struggling with developing successful relationships with others. They may be rule followers who are unable to adjust or adapt to new social situations. They need intensive instruction in developing social thinking skills and the ability to understand things from the perspective of another person. These are children who need to learn appropriate ways to initiate interactions with others appropriately, to begin and end conversations, to share speaking time, and to interpret complex, but subtle, body language. They also need instruction in understanding the perspective of others.

On the following pages, we present the framework in Figure 28 in more detail to help teachers and parents assist children in improving the effectiveness of their social skills. As you become familiar with the framework, you will see that it is entirely possible to adjust it to meet the needs of any individual you are teaching. You can also read more about teaching prerequisite skills and adapting the framework for early learners in Chapter 7.

The Complete the Puzzle Framework Steps		The Teacher Will:	The Children Will:
Step 1 **PLAY**		Teach the children to play the game that requires the use of the targeted social skill.	Use the targeted social skill in a fun and engaging game.
Step 2 **TALK**		Teach the children to name the social skill and say when it should be used.	Name the skill and, given a hypothetical situation, tell when it should be used.
Step 3 **ACT**		Teach the children to demonstrate the skill in a contrived situation.	Act out the skill in a role-playing or engineered situation.
Step 4 **USE**		Teach the children to use the skill in natural settings.	Use the skill with others in a school or home setting.
Step 5 **EXPLAIN**		Teach the children the rationale for using the skill.	Say why the skill is effective in interacting with others.
Step 6 **ADJUST**		Teach the children to use flexible thinking and problem solving.	List and demonstrate an alternative action whenever the social skill is not effective.

Figure 28. The Complete The Puzzle Framework.

Preparing to Teach the Skills With the Framework

IMPORTANT PREREQUISITES

There are several important prerequisites that are necessary for success in using the framework. These include the skills of attending, waiting, following directions, talking, and taking turns. See Chapter 7 for suggested ideas to use if your children need intensive instruction in these skills.

SET THE STAGE—USING THE PUZZLE PIECES TO MOTIVATE CHILDREN

Instruction must be designed with great consideration of the concept of motivation. The Complete the Puzzle framework was designed to capitalize on the interests of children with ASD. Because many children with ASD are skilled in and enjoy completing puzzles, simply the activity of earning puzzle pieces may be reinforcing. In addition, children with ASD often like to work systematically and to finish things. Earning pieces needed to complete the puzzle not only provides token reinforcement, but it also provides a visual representation of the progress toward developing competency in the skill.

Because we are working with young children who have difficulty with social skills, it is probable that some of these children will not engage in the activities just to earn the puzzle piece or even the social praise that accompanies it. These children may need primary reinforcers as incentives to work hard at the social skills games and activities.

Before teaching, the motivating operations for each child need to be explored. Having a good understanding of what is likely to be motivating for each child is extremely important to success in this framework. It is also crucial to assess whether the consequences actually act as reinforcers (that is, increase the likelihood that the child will repeat the behavior).

It is important to begin by establishing a clear link between the puzzle pieces and primary reinforcers, using the concept of pairing. Children must see the value in earning the pieces, so puzzle pieces must be accompanied by rewards such as attention, toys, privileges, or food. For each puzzle piece to actually serve as a positive reinforcer, each child needs enough pleasant consequences to entice him to engage in the behaviors needed to earn additional puzzle pieces.

Although in the beginning, puzzle pieces should become associated with primary rewards, it is important to aim to fade tangible rewards. Food, special activities, and privileges should become associated with praise such as verbal compliments, high fives, attention from other children and adults, and other prestigious social rewards. Be careful not to fade primary rewards too fast because, as the demand increases (i.e., from the easy level of using the skill in the game to the harder levels of using the skill in the natural environment), it is likely that backup reinforcers will need to be clearly associated with earning the puzzle pieces.

Remember that pleasant consequences for one child may not be pleasant for another child. In addition, what was a positive consequence one day may not be positive on another day. And, most important of all, if the pleasant consequences do not result in the child's repetition of the behavior, those rewards (however wonderful they may seem) are not serving as positive reinforcers. Any time a child is not making progress in achieving the objectives in a particular step, pay close attention to that child's level of motivation and adjust to provide positive consequences that will actually act as reinforcers.

CHALLENGES

To assess the level of mastery on each level of a skill, we find it motivating to offer a challenge to each child. Instead of making it seem like a test, we recommend presenting it as a challenge or a mission to be accomplished. In our experiences, children often respond with determination to rise to—and even exceed—the limits of the challenge.

In order for the children to earn each puzzle piece, we would say something like, "Now, here's a challenge for you and I bet you'll be able to do it!" At the completion of the challenge, arrange a celebration where everyone claps, cheers, and gives high fives. Then, award each child a puzzle piece and let the child place it on a puzzle frame labeled with the child's name. In order to build anticipation, excitement, and motivation for working toward earning all six puzzle pieces and completing the social skills puzzle for each skill, consider providing social praise followed by tangible reinforcers from the hierarchy explained below.

HIERARCHY OF REINFORCERS FOR EARNED PUZZLE PIECES

In this hierarchy (see Figure 29), we have presented reinforcers that increase in size and duration, in direct proportion to the response effort related to each challenge. We provide examples of tangible reinforcers and activities for earning each puzzle piece. Use small, tangible rewards that can be consumed or used within a few minutes for puzzle pieces 1 and 2. Try a snack that takes a few minutes to consume or a special activity for earning puzzle pieces 3 and 4. Save longer "choice" activity times, class parties, certificates, and medals for achieving pieces 5 and 6. In all cases, emphasize the social rewards (e.g., praise, attention, standing to receive recognition) by providing them before any primary reinforcers are delivered.

Because the games and activities focus on social interaction, it is important to select reinforcers that promote interaction. For example, arrange for the children to request the type of snack from a child who is passing things around. Or, organize the situation so children have different supplies (such as napkins and cups) and, if necessary, prompt the children to request the needed items.

To individualize the hierarchy, it is important to assess what items or activities function as positive reinforcement for the children. Conduct a reinforcer survey and/or preference assessment to get more reliable information related to individual preferences.

Framework Step 1—Play

Playing with others is an important social skill for children. However, for many children with ASD, play is work—and work is play. An unstructured play session can be a frustrating and upsetting experience for some children with ASD while the structure and repetition of work tasks can be motivating for them.

We have designed this framework to start instruction with "Play." For each of the 10 social skills targeted in this book, we teach a fun and engaging game that has enough structure to be appealing to children with ASD. We believe that the creative use of games can help provide the motivation (capitalizing on the child's interest) for the child to acquire the skill and the practice (rehearsal and repetition) needed for the child to develop some fluency in using the skill. As a bonus, there are many chances to practice other social skills such as attending to what's going on, taking turns, and following directions. In addition, playing games also creates situations to shape other skills such as making comments or requests, giving directions to others, and reacting appropriately to winning and losing.

The games are designed around the typical interests of children with ASD (e.g., animals, transportation, solving mysteries, and superheroes). In addition, we have planned for the games to capitalize on the typical strengths of children with autism (e.g., completing something systematically, moving around, and following routines). Games provide a natural opportunity for repetition of a skill, making the practice more fun than repeating isolated drills. Therefore Step 1 is Play and involves the children actually playing the game.

It is tempting to provide big rewards for winning the game, but it is more important to save these rewards for earning the puzzle pieces. Although the concept of winning and losing may be motivating to some children, if the consequences of winning or losing are too great, the focus on the skill itself is lost. Take care in using the idea of motivating children by comparing their

Social Praise and Token Reinforcement	Ideas for Tangible Reinforcers for Pairing
Earning Puzzle Piece #1: Social praise such as claps, cheers, and high fives followed by ⟶	Small pieces of wrapped candy, stickers, stamps, crackers, pretzels, one cookie, a little music or singing (one song), sensory activities (short period of jumping or swinging)
Earning Puzzle Piece #2: Social praise such as claps, cheers, and high fives followed by ⟶	Small prize from a "treasure box" (i.e., whistle, pencil, small pack of candy) or small snack (i.e., apple, two cookies, or small bag of pretzels or chips), music (two or three songs), short recess period
Earning Puzzle Piece #3: Social praise such as claps, cheers, and high fives followed by ⟶	Bigger prize from a "treasure box" (i.e., box of crayons, small packaged toy), special snack (i.e., cookies and juice, cup of fruit, popcorn, package of cheese crackers), listening to favorite music and dancing (as a group), or bringing an item from home to play with and share
Earning Puzzle Piece #4: Social praise such as claps, cheers, and high fives followed by ⟶	Choosing a "fun time" activity for 10 minutes (i.e., computer games, board games, outside time); icing, decorating and eating cookies; painting or other art project; taking a walk around the school to show off puzzle pieces
Earning Puzzle Piece #5: Social praise such as claps, cheers, and high fives followed by ⟶	Medium treasure box item or surprise item in a bag, including art supplies, card games, puzzles, or stickers of TV characters; activities such as picking a friend to sit beside at lunch; 20 minutes of "fun time" with a computer game, reading, or playing a game with a friend
Earning Puzzle Piece #6: Social praise such as claps, cheers, and high fives followed by ⟶	Culminating activity or party (i.e., pizza party, party with cupcakes and ice cream, extra recess time, popcorn and movie party), ceremonies for passing out badges (perhaps inviting peer buddies or parents), medals and/or certificates, taking pictures with completed puzzles and certificates

Figure 29. Hierarchy of reinforcers for earned puzzle pieces.

performances to others. However, it can be effective to help children compete against their own previous performances. Remember that games:

- are fun and can be designed with relatively low demand conditions;
- are naturally social and include multiple opportunities to interact with others;
- can motivate children to practice specific social skills to gain fluency;
- offer structure and predictability that can be comforting to children with ASD;
- have a built-in finished concept that motivates children to complete the game;
- can focus on multiple skills at one time, mimicking natural environment conditions;
- include emotions (e.g., happy about winning, sad about losing) and opportunities to recognize and manage emotions; and
- provide opportunities to recognize and respond to the perspective of others (e.g., congratulate winners and show empathy for losers).

At the end of Step 1, issue a challenge to determine if children can play the game fluently and independently. Give children a puzzle piece, as shown in the photo.

Framework Step 2—Talk

In Step 2, teach the children to name the skill, to say when the skill should be used, and to recognize situations in which the skill will be necessary. For each skill, we provide specific directions and detailed examples of how to provide this instruction. We give descriptions for using such methods as direct instruction, Discrete Trial Training, and/or Discrimination Training and show examples of how to provide visual supports for teaching this. At the end of Step 2, we describe examples of challenges that you can issue to determine if children have met mastery at this level.

Framework Step 3—Act

The puzzle framework was developed around the need for many children with ASD to have multiple opportunities to practice skills. We provide details on how to set up role-plays and provide opportunities for so that children will have the opportunity to become fluent in the use of the skill in many different situations. We provide examples of practice in multiple settings with different people and different materials. At the end of Step 3, we include instructions and examples so you can issue a challenge to determine if children have mastered the skill at this level.

Framework Step 4—Use

The framework takes into account the need for precise planning and instruction to help children to generalize their skills. Not only do children with ASD need role-plays and behavioral rehearsals, but they also need opportunities to use the skill in their natural environment. We provide information on continuing to teach in the natural environment, not expecting skills to automatically transfer from the use of the skill in contrived situations. We explain the use of activity-based instruction, incidental teaching, Pivotal Response Training, and other naturalistic teaching methods to provide opportunities for children to generalize the skill to the natural setting. We also provide reminders of the importance of making sure the children have positive reinforcement for using the skill across settings, particularly through self-awareness and self-management. At the end of Step 4, we explain ways to issue challenges to determine if children have met mastery at this level.

Framework Step 5—Explain

In Step 5, we provide instructions for teaching children to explain the importance of the social skill and why it helps them have successful social interactions. In our experience, children who understand the why of social behaviors are more likely to use appropriate social skills. In this step, we teach the child the connections between thinking, feeling, and behaving. We show examples of how to provide instruction in self-awareness, self-management, Social Thinking, and other cognitive behavioral interventions. At the end of Step 5, we have examples of how you might issue a challenge to determine if children have met mastery at this level.

Framework Step 6—Adjust

Lastly, the framework includes the need for children to learn flexible thinking and problem-solving skills. Many children with ASD are excellent rule followers. Once taught a skill, procedure, or guideline, many children with ASD will stick extremely closely to the way they were taught. This sometimes results in such rigid thinking and acting that it interferes with social relationships. These children sometimes appoint themselves as overseers of others, creating difficulties as they persistently point out those who aren't following the rule, seeing a rule as a law more than a suggestion or guideline. They often persist in doing something exactly the same way even if it is not working. We provide suggestions for specific instruction to help children learn flexibility (try another way) and tolerance (it's okay if others don't always do it this way.) At the end of Step 6, we show examples designed to help you issue a challenge to determine if children have demonstrated mastery of the skill at this, the highest, level.

In Chapter 6, we start by taking the first social skill, "Asking Politely," through each of the six steps of the framework. Following this detailed explanation of the first skill, we'll describe the games, activities, and challenges for each of the other nine skills. Please note that the 10 sample skills provided in this book should definitely not be considered a complete social skills curriculum, but can be used in conjunction with more complete curriculum guides such as the ABLLS®-R and VB-MAPP. Also, remember that in the last chapter, we will provide information on teaching prerequisite skills for early learners.

CHAPTER 6

The 10 Skills and the Games and Activities

Skill #1: Asking Politely

STEP 1

Play—Earning the First Puzzle Piece With the Lotto Game

Framework Step	The Teacher Will:	The Children Will:
Step 1 **PLAY**	Teach the children to play the game that requires the use of the targeted social skill.	Use the targeted social skill in a fun and engaging game.

Use the game Lotto to teach the skill of asking politely. To set up the game:
1. Give each child a Lotto card.
2. Give the children some of the matching pieces for the cards of the other players.
3. Make sure the children don't have the pieces that match their own card.

Directions for play. To play the game:
1. Direct children to look at their board and the pieces in front of them. (They should not have any matches.)
2. Instruct them to look at the pieces in front of the other children and to take turns politely asking their friends for the pieces they need.
3. Tell the children to continue taking turns making requests until at least one board is covered with its matching pieces.
4. Explain that when a board is covered, the winner calls out, "I'm finished!"

Variations. Several variations can be made, including:
- Boards of 4 to 25 (or even more) can be created depending on the level of the children.
- Lotto cards can be pictures, letters, numbers, words, symbols, or signs.
- Pieces can be exact matches or can be written words to match to pictures.
- Games with new pictures can be used to expand vocabulary as well.

Teaching the game. For quick learners or experienced players, explain:

We're going to play a game called "Lotto" and you are the players. Your goal is to get all of the pieces you need to match each picture on your board. The first person to cover up every picture with a match is the winner. Start by looking at the pictures your friends have. They will have the matching pieces for your board. So when it's your turn, call one friend by name and nicely ask for a piece by saying something like, "Hey Will, could I have the train, please?" When someone asks you for a match, you should say something like, "Sure, here you go!" or "Yes, you can have the train!"

For early learners or new players, explain: "You are the players. Your goal is to get all of the pieces you need to cover up your board with matching pictures. Watch this."

Demonstration. Provide directions and a model such as this: "Look everyone, I need a picture of a helicopter, and Kylee has it. So, I'll say, 'Kylee, can I please have the helicopter?'"
Create a dialogue with the students as you play, with suggestions such as:
- So let's practice. We'll each take a turn to look at the boards of our friends.
- Kylee, look at your board and now look at Mariah's pictures. What pictures does she have?
- Right! She has some of your transportation pieces.
- What picture does she have that you want?
- Terrific! She does have a train picture, so, now say, "Mariah, can I please have the train?"

Practice a few rounds individually and then start the game. Remind the children of the rules: "Your job is to ask politely for the pieces you need to fill your board with matches. Keep looking at the pieces your friends have, so you can ask them for your matching pieces." Play the game many times, giving the children plenty of opportunities to make requests.

Challenge for Step 1. The test is to see if each child can play the game independently. Tell students,

Okay, we've been working on playing a game called "Lotto" and I have a challenge for you! It's your challenge to play an entire game without any help from me! Everyone who plays the game without any help will get the first puzzle piece for your own puzzle chart! And, guess what? Everyone who gets a first puzzle piece also gets a cookie!

Celebration Ceremony for Step 1. Provide a celebration ceremony by handing children their puzzle pieces to put on their own puzzle frames. Make sure there are plenty of opportunities for clapping, cheering, and giving "high fives!" Select accompanying tangible reinforcers such as the samples listed in the Hierarchy of Reinforcers (see p. "Figure 29. Hierarchy of reinforcers for earned puzzle pieces." on page 79).

STEP 2
Talk—Earning the Second Puzzle Piece

Once the children can play the game successfully, set up a series of group discussions to teach the children to name the skill and say when it should be used. Some children will be able to participate in a discussion without additional teaching. In this case, use questioning techniques to keep the discussion on track. Use the suggestions below as a guide for the topics you discuss.

Framework Step		The Teacher Will:	The Children Will:
Step 2 TALK		Teach the children to name the social skill and say when it should be used.	Name the skill and, given a hypothetical situation, tell when it should be used.

Other children may need more direct and explicit teaching. To do this, you can lead a discussion such as this: "Hey everyone! Remember that game we played called "Lotto?" Tell me what you did in that game." Provide positive reinforcement such as recognition, praise, tokens, or treats for answers such as:

- "We matched pictures."
- "We got pictures from our partners."
- "We filled up our boards."
- "We asked our friends for pictures."

Prompt these answers if necessary by using strategies designed to teach verbal exchanges. For example, hold up a board and say, "We matched _____" while pointing to the pictures on the board. Or "We got pictures from _____" while pointing to some of the other children. As always, when teaching intraverbals, practice enough so you can fade the visual supports until you have a completely verbal exchange (i.e., a verbal question and verbal response without the use of pictures).

Then ask, "How did you get your matching pictures?" If necessary, shape answers such as "We asked our friends," "We asked for them," or "We said 'please.'"

Summarize your discussion by saying something like:

When we played the game, we were using social skills. The name of the social skill we're going to talk about today is "asking politely." This is an important skill because it's a skill that helps you get things you need or want. If you want or need something, you should ask for it politely.

Use Discrete Trial Training techniques to provide continuous practice with the skill by asking, "What are some ways to ask politely?" Prompt and reinforce answers such as:

- "Can I please have a turn?"
- "May I have more juice, please?"
- "May I play with that?"
- "Could you help me, please?"

Provide good models for appropriate inflection and tone of voice. For some children, you may want to add a bit of Discrimination Training. In this case, you might first use an appropriate tone, volume, cadence, and inflection, saying, "Can I please have a turn?" Then, ask the children if that sounds like a polite request. Reinforce their "yes" answers. Next, ask the question in a loud and demanding tone, asking them if that sounds like a polite request. Reinforce their "no" answers. Here are some examples for Discrimination Training to help children distinguish between polite and impolite requests.

These requests are polite	These requests are not polite
"May I please have that?"	"Give me that!"
"I want it, please."	"I want it!"
"Could you get that, please?"	"Go get that for me."
"Would you please do it?"	"Do it!"

If necessary, use visual support techniques or an Incredible 5-Point Scale as a visual for their tone and volume of voice—and do this as often as necessary to get immediate and correct responses. Then, provide Discrete Trial Training practice with the skill by asking repeated similar questions, such as:

Teacher: What's the name of our skill?
Children: Asking politely.
Teacher: You're right!

Teacher: So, if you need more milk at dinner, what should you do?
Children: Ask for it politely.
Teacher: You're right!

Teacher: If you want a turn with a toy, what should you do?
Children: Ask for it politely.
Teacher: That's a great idea!

Teacher: When you want a special treat, what should you do?
Children: Ask for it politely.
Teacher: Terrific answer!

Continue these interactions, rotating among the four questions above at a high rate. Alternate group and individual responses, require a high level of participation, and arrange for a high level of success. Provide enough opportunities so that the responses become fluent, but make it fun. Once the routine is set, distribute practice over time, interjecting a question on another topic, such as "What are you having for lunch today?" or "What time do you go to gym?" Then, go back to questions such as:

Teacher: So, if you need help with a project, what should you do?
Children: Ask for it politely.
Teacher: Awesome idea!

Make sure the children can give examples of polite requests. Periodically, include questions such as:

Teacher: How would you politely ask for milk?
Children: May I have some milk, please?

Teacher: How would you politely ask for a turn?
Children: Could I please have a turn?

Teacher: How would you ask politely for attention?
Children: Could we play this game together?

When children have demonstrated mastery (met a criterion such as correctly answering on the first attempt of a new session for 3 days in a row), set up a challenge for each individual. Distribute these as tests throughout the day so that you make sure children are not repeating answers they have just heard.

Challenge for Step 2. The test is to make sure each child can name the skill and describe when it should be used. Set up a time to be with each individual child for an interaction such as this sample teacher script.

Teacher: Okay, we've been working on a social skill and I have a challenge for you! We played a game and you had a Lotto board with pictures and you used a social skill to get matching pictures from your friends. Your challenge is to name that social skill!
Student: Asking politely!
Teacher: Great! And, if you want a toy that's high up on a shelf in someone else's house, what should you do?
Student: Ask for it politely!
Teacher: What would you say?
Student: Can I please play with that toy?
Teacher: What else could you say?
Student: Can I see that toy, please?

Celebration Ceremony for Step 2. Provide a celebration ceremony by handing children their puzzle pieces to put on their puzzles. Make sure there are plenty of opportunities for clapping, cheering, and giving high fives. Select accompanying tangible reinforcers such as the samples listed in the Hierarchy of Reinforcers. In some cases, it may seem unnecessary to provide such a big celebration, but with many children with ASD, motivation to interact socially is a challenge. And there are more challenging tasks to come, so setting up the routine of celebrating can increase the chances that children will make good efforts to work on the more difficult tasks.

STEP 3
Act—Earning the Third Puzzle Piece

When the children can name the skill and say when it should be used, set up a series of role-plays. If possible, set up the role-plays like scenes in a television show or movie. You might want to have a real (or pretend) video camera on hand to motivate the children.

Framework Step	The Teacher Will:	The Children Will:
Step 3 ACT	Teach the children to demonstrate the skill in an engineered situation.	Act out the skill in a role-playing or engineered situation.

Set up the situation like this: "Hi, friends! Remember the social skill called 'asking politely?' We're going to practice that skill and you'll get to be the actors—just like on television!" Practice scenes such as the ones below, switching roles among the children.

Actor 1: *Sits at the table with a toy helicopter.*
Actor 2: *Comes up to Actor 1.* Can I see the helicopter, please?
Actor 1: Sure—here you go!
Actor 2: Thanks! *Plays with the helicopter.*

Actor 1: *Pours juice into a cup.*
Actor 2: *Comes up to Actor 1.* May I have some juice, please?
Actor 1: Sure. Here's a cup for you!
Actor 2: Thanks! *Drinks the juice.*

Actors 1, 2, and 3: *Play with a train set.*
Actor 4: *Comes up to them.* Can I play with you?
Actors 1, 2, and 3: Sure. Come sit down!
Actor 4: Thanks! *Joins the play.*

If possible, take pictures and review the pictures, or video the role-plays and watch them as movies. To enhance the experience, add titles to the videos or photos such as "Asking Politely! Starring John and Friends."

Coach the children to use various ways of making polite requests and ask them for their ideas for role-plays. Provide modeling to help them add appropriate intonation and body language into their actions. Some examples of polite requests include:

- "Can I please have a turn?"
- "Could I please play with that?"
- "Could you help me, please?"
- "May I have more juice, please?"

Use activity-based instruction and incidental teaching techniques to contrive some situations to see if the children will use the skill in a more natural situation. For example, set up a group of children playing with LEGOs™ while one child is out of the room. When the child comes back to the room, wait to see if the child goes to ask for a turn. If not, use least-to-most prompting to help the child ask a question such as the ones on the previous page. As often as possible, engineer the environment to give children opportunities to use the skill.

When children have demonstrated mastery, set up a test for each individual child. Make sure to distribute these tests throughout the day so that you make sure children are not just repeating answers they have just heard.

Challenge for Step 3. The test is to make sure each child can act out the skill in a role-play situation. For example, set up a time to be with each individual child for an interaction. Tell the student, "Your challenge is to act out this social skill in a movie! We'll make a tape of you asking politely on the playground. Then, we'll look at your movies on the screen!" Use scenarios like these:

- Your friends are playing on the swings, and it is your movie role to figure out a good way to get a turn.
- Your friends are playing ball, and it is your movie role to figure out a good way to play with them.

Celebration Ceremony for Step 3. When the children have demonstrated proficient use of the social skill, provide a celebration ceremony by handing children their puzzle pieces to put on their puzzles. Have an accompanying party and continue to praise their success at earning puzzle piece #3. Be sure to provide a big celebration and continue pairing the puzzle pieces with plenty of social praise and treats. To improve the chances that children will make good efforts to work on future tasks, make sure that the rewards are escalating as the demand is increasing. Keep observing closely to make sure the rewards are truly acting as reinforcers (i.e., increasing the chance that the child will use the skills).

STEP 4

Use—Earning the Fourth Puzzle Piece

Framework Step	The Teacher Will:	The Children Will:
Step 4 **USE**	Teach the children to use the skill in natural settings.	Use the skill with others in a school or home setting.

Using joint action routines and incidental teaching techniques, engineer opportunities for children to use the skill in the natural environment like the following:

- take away the basket of straws when the children are going through the lunch line, creating an opportunity for the children to ask politely for a straw;
- put a stack of cups on the table, but act as if you are going to pour the juice right onto the table, creating an opportunity for children to ask for a cup; and
- put favorite books, movies, or other items in closets or on high shelves, creating opportunities for children to ask for them.

Be sure to provide descriptive feedback when children make polite requests. Examples are, "Sure, thanks for asking so politely" or "Wow, I love helping when you ask so nicely!" When children don't make polite requests, withhold the item and use intraverbals to provide corrective feedback. For example, "You want a cup, _____?" providing an opportunity for the child to add please. Or, provide a reminder such as, "What's a more polite way to ask?" When the children can use the skill reliably in role-plays and some contrived situations in natural settings, set up a discussion such as the following: "Okay, movie stars! Remember making movies with the social skill of asking politely? What kinds of things happened in those movies?"

Expect answers like, "We asked for turns playing with toys" and "We asked for juice and cookies at snack." Follow up with, "And, what were some of the ways that you asked?" Students may answer with, "Can I have a turn, please?" or "May I please have some juice?"

Some suggestions for increasing the chance children will use the skill include:

- Post visual supports in the room to remind children to use the social skill of the week.
- Review pictures of the role-plays or watch videos of the social skill.
- Post the token economy chart for each child in a place that's easy to see.
- Keep the puzzle framework in clear view.
- Bring in lots of new items such as a musical instrument, plants to water, animals to pet, or pictures to see.
- Create communication temptations such as putting favorite toys in containers that are difficult to open.
- Use a self-management chart like the one in Figure 30 to help each child monitor his or her own progress.

Challenge for Step 4. The test is to see if each child can use the skill in natural settings. For example, set up an interaction such as in this sample teacher script.

"I asked politely!"

What I wanted:	What I said:

Figure 30. Self-management chart.

Now, here's the challenge for puzzle piece #4. I am going to watch you all week long and look for you to show me that you know how to ask for things politely! We'll use our chart to keep track of how many polite requests you make this week. When you have 10 polite requests, you'll earn puzzle piece #4!

Use tokens that seem appropriate and motivating for your children. You might use stickers, happy faces, coins, chips, high-five signs, or a token economy chart such as the one in Figure 31.

Celebration Ceremony for Step 4. When the children have completed their charts, provide a celebration ceremony to hand children their puzzle pieces to put on their puzzles. Make sure you are emphasizing social praise by clapping, cheering, and giving high fives all around the room, along with providing reinforcers. Remember, there are still more challenging tasks to come, so keep working to make sure that the rewards are escalating as the demand is increasing. And, don't forget to keep observing closely to make sure the rewards are truly acting as reinforcers.

STEP 5

Explain—Earning the Fifth Puzzle Piece

When the children are using the social skill in the natural environment, start discussions related to why is it good to ask for things politely. Use Social Stories™ and Social Thinking® strategies to teach children about expected and unexpected behaviors.

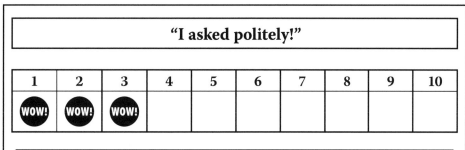

"I asked politely!"

1	2	3	4	5	6	7	8	9	10
WOW!	WOW!	WOW!							

Figure 31. Token economy chart.

Framework Step	The Teacher Will:	The Children Will:
Step 5 EXPLAIN	Teach the children the rationale for using the skill.	Say why the skill is effective in interacting with others.

Write and discuss a Social Story™ such as the following:

Asking For Things Politely

Sometimes people want to ask for things. This might be something that you can eat or drink, like a cookie or some juice. Or, it might be something that you can play with, like an iPad or a computer. There are also times that people want to ask to do something like go to a movie or for a ride in the car.

Usually, people ask for things politely. That means they use nice words like "please" and "can I?" It also means using a nice tone of voice, so it sounds like a question and not a command. They also use an inside voice, one that's loud enough to be heard by someone standing close, but not loud enough to be heard outside the room.

When people ask for things politely, they are more likely to get it. This doesn't always happen, but it usually makes others happy when people talk politely. When people use rude words and yell, the other people may feel mad or sad. I will try to ask for things politely.

Use Social Thinking® strategies to explain the following:

When you want other people to do something for you or to give you something, they expect you to use nice words in a polite tone of voice. They will be surprised if you ask for something by yelling or demanding it. If you ask in a rude way, they might have weird thoughts about you because this is not expected, and they might not be willing to give you what you want.

Challenge for Step 5. The test is to see if each child can say why the skill is important. For example, set up a time to be with each individual child for an interaction such as this:

> Okay, we've been working on a social skill, and I have a challenge for you! Your challenge is to explain why it's good to ask for things politely. All day long, I'll be looking for chances to talk to you. When I do, I might ask you some questions about why it's important to be polite. I'll keep track on my own chart and when you have 10 good answers, you'll have met your challenge! Be prepared with some good answers!

Celebration Ceremony for Step 5. When the children have passed this test, provide a celebration ceremony by handing children their puzzle pieces to put on their puzzles. Have an accompanying party and continue to praise their success at earning puzzle piece #5. Keep making the celebrations bigger and better as children master the more difficult challenges. Emphasize the social aspect of the celebration, but remember to keep pairing social rewards with more tangible rewards.

STEP 6

Adjust—Earning the Sixth Puzzle Piece

When the children have earned puzzle pieces for demonstrating the skill in the natural environment and can explain the reasons for using the skill, start a discussion such as the one below on adjusting when the skill isn't working. Use some of the ideas from the sections on Social Thinking® or Cognitive Behavior Modification.

Framework Step	The Teacher Will:	The Children Will:
Step 6 ADJUST	Teach the children to use flexible thinking and problem solving.	List and demonstrate an alternative action whenever the social skill is not effective.

Start off by prompting the students with "Hi scholars! Let's review that social skill called 'asking politely.' What are some good things to say to get things you want?" Expect answers like:

- Please. May I?
- Would you?
- Could you?
- Can I please?

Follow up by asking children: "What happens if that doesn't work?" If necessary, shape such answers as:
- I could ask again.
- I could ask later.
- I could ask someone else.
- I could do something else for a while.

Provide reinforcement such as "Those are great answers!" Then, extend the learning by sharing the following:

Let me tell you something new! It's important to think about other people. Sometimes other people are busy. Sometimes other people are not able to help. Sometimes other people don't want to help. Sometimes people are mad. Sometimes people are sad. It's a good idea to think about the other person before asking for help. For example, consider the following situations:
- If your mom is cooking dinner and stirring hot soup on the stove, is it a good time to ask for help opening a package?
- If your dad is up on a ladder, cleaning leaves out of the gutter, is it a good time to ask him to fix your toy?
- If your friend is crying because a toy is broken, is it a good time to ask for a favor?
- If your friend is mad because something won't work, is it a good time to ask for help?

These might be times to look for someone else to ask for what you want. Or, it might be a good idea to ask that person at a later time. What are some things you should look for before asking?
- If the person has tears.
- If the person is busy doing something else.
- If the person's face has a frown.
- If the person is mad.

If those things happen, what should you do?
- Ask that person at a later time.
- Look for someone else to ask for what you want.
- Do something else for a while.
- Ask for something else for a while.

Include a consequence map as a visual support for these discussions.

Challenge for Step 6. The test is to see if each child can use problem-solving skills and flexible thinking related to asking for things politely. Tell students: "Now, here's the challenge for puzzle piece #6. I am going to give each of you a blank consequence map. You'll fill it in to show me that you know how to solve problems and use flexible thinking."

Set up a series of consequence maps with situations such as the following:

- You have a new computer game, but you need someone to show you how to get started. Your brother is busy with his homework and even though you asked politely, he said, "no."
- Your friend is playing with his new train set, and you want a turn. You said, "Please, please can I have a turn," and he said, "I want to play by myself."
- You are thirsty, and the juice is on the top shelf of the refrigerator.
- You and your mom are visiting your cousins, and they have a swimming pool.

Celebration Ceremony for Step 6. When the children have passed this last test, provide the biggest celebration yet. Hand children their puzzle pieces to put on their puzzles and take a picture of each child with his or her completed puzzle frame. Have an accompanying party and continue to praise their success at completing the entire puzzle. Emphasize the social aspect of the celebration, perhaps inviting peer buddies, other teachers, or parents to the celebration.

Skill #2: Responding to Directions From Friends

STEP 1

Play—Earning the First Puzzle Piece With Simon Says

Framework Step		The Teacher Will:	The Children Will:
Step 1 PLAY		Teach the children to play the game that requires the use of the targeted social skill.	Use the targeted social skill in a fun and engaging game.

Use an adapted version of the game Simon Says to teach the skill of following directions from friends. To set up the game, arrange the children in a semicircle and designate a spot for Simon to stand.

Directions for play. To play the game:

1. Pick a person to play Simon.
2. Tell Simon to take five turns giving directions.
3. Instruct the children to follow the directions that Simon gives.
4. Take turns until every child has been Simon.

Teaching the game. Use Discrete Trial Training to give children practice in following directions quickly. Provide a choice board like that in Figure 32 to help Simon give directions quickly.

Explain to the children that, prior to playing the game, they need to pick Simon. A sample way for picking Simon is to give each child a number and place matching numbers in a bag. For the first turn, draw out a number and appoint the child who has the matching number as the first Simon. Subsequently, let the current Simon pick the number from the bag to choose the next Simon.

Explain to the children that each Simon will have five turns to give directions. To keep up with the number of turns for Simon, it is helpful to put a checkmark on the board by each number as a direction is given (see Figure 33). Design a chart like that in Figure 33 to keep up with the number of directions each child has followed. For example, after Liam has played the role of Simon and given directions, the other children mark their chart for following directions. The same process follows for each child.

Provide exciting rewards to all children who complete their charts. Post the charts on the wall and celebrate "following directions from friends"!

Variations. If you have experienced players or quick learners, you may consider playing the traditional version of the game by having the children only follow the directions when Simon says to do so. However, the point of the game is to provide practice following directions from peers, so avoid playing this way if it distracts from the major purpose.

Challenge for Step 1. Tell students,

We have played Simon Says and practiced following directions from our friends. Now, here is our challenge! You're going to play that game all by yourselves, and I'm just going to watch. For this game, each Simon will only give two directions and then will pull the number for the next Simon. Everyone who follows directions from all of the Simons will get the first puzzle piece!

When each child has met the challenge, provide a celebration ceremony similar to that described in Step 1 of Skill #1.

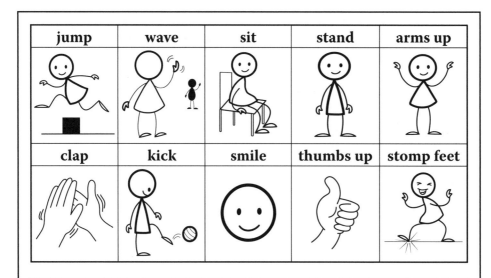

Figure 32. Simon Says choice board.

Simon's Turn
✓
✓
✓
✓
✓

I Followed Directions From Simon!				
Liam	Simon	✗	✗	✗
Wyatt	✗	Simon	✗	✗
Addie	✗	✗	Simon	
Landrey	✗	✗	✗	Simon	
Campbell	✗	✗	✗		Simon

Figure 33. Simon Says recording charts.

STEP 2

Talk—Earning the Second Puzzle Piece

Framework Step		The Teacher Will:	The Children Will:
Step 2 TALK		Teach the children to name the social skill and say when it should be used.	Name the skill and, given a hypothetical situation, tell when it should be used.

Begin the discussion by saying, "Let's talk about what we did when we played Simon Says." You might ask children questions such as, "What happened when Simon was in front of the group?" If necessary, provide prompts for the children by showing them the choice board and reminding them of the actions performed by the leader:

- Remember when Jamie said, "stand up"?
- Do you recall when Julie said, "jump"?
- Think about how Fred told us to sit down.
- Remember how George told us to wave?

Reinforce responses immediately with descriptive feedback such as, "What did you do when Simon gave a direction?" Expect or teach answers like:

- I did it!
- I followed the directions.
- Fred said jump, so I jumped.
- I did what Emily told me!

Follow up with a question like, "So, what do you think we were learning in this game, Simon Says?" Expect or teach answers such as:

- Doing what people tell us.
- Listen to what people tell us and do it.
- Following directions from friends.
- Do what somebody says to do.

Provide positive feedback like, "That is right, we were following directions from our friends. That's our new social skill!" Use Discrete Trial Training to provide opportunities for the children to identify the skill. Use scenarios such as the following:

- While building a castle, George told Gina to put the red block on top of the castle.

- While drawing, Hannah drew a cake and she told Carly to draw the candles.

Follow up by asking students, "What should the friend do?" Expect answers such as "Put the red block on top of the castle" and "Draw a candle." Then, ask students to name the skill ("following directions from friends") by responding with, "What is this called?"

Consider providing more scenarios until the children are able to respond quickly. An alternative to asking the question is to provide opportunities to finish a sentence or fill in the blank. Ask children: "So, when are some times that you might follow directions from friends?" Shape answers such as:

- When they want me to help with something.
- When they want to play a game or make something.

Then, say, "Give me an example of when you would follow a friend's instructions." Reinforce any response that represents an appropriate time for a child to follow directions from a peer.

Challenge for Step 2. Tell students they have a new challenge:

This is to see if you can name our new social skill and tell when it should be used! I'll be watching all week long for a chance to ask you some questions. I'll keep a record and when you have correctly answered five questions, you will have met the challenge!

Give a scenario and then ask questions such as:

- o Joe wanted paper towels, but the cabinet door would not stay open. Joe told Julie to hold open the door. What skill was Julie using?
- o Ellen wanted to play a game on the computer. She told Paul to open the game on the computer. What should Paul do? What skill was he using?

Follow up by asking students, "So, when should you follow directions from friends?" Expect an answer like, "When our friends tell us they need help or when our friends want us to do something." When each child has met the challenge, provide a celebration ceremony similar to the one described in Step 2 of Skill #1.

STEP 3
Act—Earning the Third Puzzle Piece

Framework Step	The Teacher Will:	The Children Will:
Step 3 ACT	Teach the children to demonstrate the skill in an engineered situation.	Act out the skill in a role-playing or engineered situation.

Set up behavioral rehearsals and explain to the children that they will be pretending to be in a movie or TV show. Set up scripts for role-plays that include the children's interests. Pair each child with a peer. Prior to the role-play, review the cue cards for the social skill (see Figure 34). Say something like: "Hi, friends! Today we're going to make a movie. I have some scripts here, and you'll get to choose your own costumes and props. Our movies will show you following directions from friends!"

Set up two scenes for the children. Scene 1 should be costumes with many pieces and props for a pirate and ship. Challenges for the students in this scene could be "Please help me put on the pirate shirt" or "Put the gold coins in the treasure chest." Scene 2 should have princess clothes and a castle made of blocks. Here, have students direct peers to "Put the blocks here to make the castle" or "Hide behind the castle; I'll rescue you."

Use the steps in the cue card to review role-plays. The conversation may go like this:

Teacher: When the pirate asked for help, what did _____ do first?
Children: Looked at him.
Teacher: Fantastic! What did he do next?
Children: He listened to what the pirate said.
Teacher: You got it! Then?
Children: He helped him put on the costume.
Teacher: Outstanding! So, what did he do?
Children: Followed the pirate's directions!
Teacher: Hooray!

Using activity-based instruction, set up opportunities for children to take turns giving and following directions. Say something like, "Go with your partner to each station as indicated on your schedule. There will be directions for each activity. One person will tell the other person what to do. Sometimes you'll give directions and sometimes you'll follow directions." Set up these stations:

Following Directions From a Friend	
look	Look at your friend.
listen	Listen to your friend.
do	Do what your friend asked.

Figure 34. Cue card.

- *Drawing*: Children take turns following directions on how to draw something, such as an airplane, a pirate ship, a rainbow, or a princess castle.
- *LEGO™ Blocks*: Children take turns following directions on how to build something, such as a Barbie™ castle, robot, or space station.
- *Puzzle*: Children take turns following directions on how to complete the puzzle (i.e., "Start with the corner pieces; now, get the edge pieces; you do the sky").

Challenge for Step 3: Tell students,

Hi everyone! You've been doing great with following directions from friends. So, here is your challenge for Step 3. Look, we have part of a robot here! We need to help complete it. I have a bucket of instructions that we need to follow to finish this robot. You can each take a turn to pick one of the instructions and read it to your friend. We'll watch and see if your friend follows your instructions!

Consider instructions such as the following:
- Put the hat on the robot's head.
- Put the two robot eyes on his head.
- Cover the robot's arms with aluminum foil.

When each child has met the challenge, provide a celebration ceremony similar to the one in Step 3 of Skill #1.

STEP 4
Use—Earning the Fourth Puzzle Piece

Framework Step		The Teacher Will:	The Children Will:
Step 4 **USE**		Teach the children to use the skill in natural settings.	Use the skill with others in a school or home setting.

Use incidental teaching techniques to create opportunities that will require children to follow directions. For instance, perhaps a child loves *Star Wars* but can't put together the pieces to make a *Star Wars* spaceship. Set up an activity that would allow the child to complete the project by following the directions from a peer.

In addition, watch for opportunities to use social praise and to provide token reinforcement for following directions from friends. Make a chart to keep track and post the chart in a prominent place in the room. Periodically remind the children that you are watching! When children do follow directions, make an announcement and provide the token. For example, say, "Jerry gets a sticker! He followed Lisa's directions by putting the book on the shelf." Then give Jerry the sticker.

When appropriate, provide corrective feedback, such as, "Wait! Henry, what did Jim ask you to do? Did you follow his direction? What could you try next time?" If necessary, pair your verbal feedback with a cue card that shows what happened and what students can try next time (see Figure 35).

Challenge for Step 4. Tell students their challenge is to follow instructions from their friends: "Today, I'll be looking, and every time I see you following directions, I will place a sticker on your chart. When you have five stickers, you'll get puzzle piece #4!" When each child has met the challenge, provide a celebration ceremony similar to the one in Step 4 of Skill #1.

What Happened
My friend asked for help getting our snack.
I didn't listen to my friend. I was busy.
We didn't get to eat our snack.
What I Can Try Next Time
I can try to stop and listen.
I can listen and help my friend.
We can eat our snack together!

Figure 35. Cue card to assist in providing feedback.

STEP 5

Explain—Earning the Fifth Puzzle Piece

Framework Step	The Teacher Will:	The Children Will:
Step 5 **EXPLAIN**	Teach the children the rationale for using the skill.	Say why the skill is effective in interacting with others.

Use Social Thinking® strategies to help the children learn to explain why it is important to follow directions from friends. Discuss behaviors that are typically expected when giving and following directions. Then discuss unexpected behaviors and teach the children to discriminate between them with a T-chart (see Figure 36).

Discuss the potential reactions of others to unexpected behaviors, including:

- Others get mad.
- They don't want to be friends.
- They don't ask me again.
- They think I'm weird.

Use another graphic organizer to help children list some reasons why they think it is important to follow directions from their friends. As children work on their graphic organizers, shape answers such as:

- Your friends might need help.
- You want to please your friend.
- You don't know how to do something.
- You want to learn something new.

Expected Behaviors	Unexpected Behaviors
Following the direction	Ignoring your friend
Doing what your friend said to do	Walking away from your friend
Politely saying that you don't want to do it	Doing something else instead

Figure 36. T-chart for discriminating behaviors.

Challenge for Step 5. Tell students,

You have been working hard at following directions from friends. Today's challenge is to create a consequence map so that we can see if you can explain why it's good to follow directions from friends and what can possibly happen if you don't.

Have students pick one of the following situations and complete a chart like the one in Figure 37:
- Bridgett told you to help her pick up the books she dropped.
- Mason provided directions for you to finish building the tower.
- Samuel told you to bring the balls out to the playground.

When each child has met the challenge, provide a celebration ceremony similar to the one in Step 5 of Skill #1.

STEP 6

Adjust—Earning the Sixth Puzzle Piece

Framework Step	The Teacher Will:	The Children Will:
Step 6 ADJUST	Teach the children to use flexible thinking and problem solving.	List and demonstrate an alternative action whenever the social skill is not effective.

Start a discussion with the children such as, "We have learned a lot about following directions. One thing we have not talked about is making a good decision

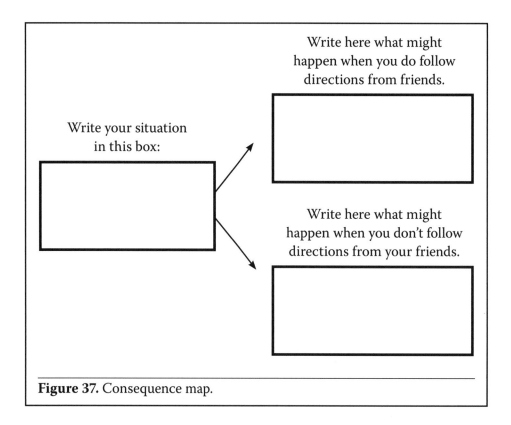

Write here what might happen when you do follow directions from friends.

Write your situation in this box:

Write here what might happen when you don't follow directions from your friends.

Figure 37. Consequence map.

when thinking about following directions from friends. Let's read this Social Story™ and talk about making decisions."

Deciding When to Follow Directions From Friends

At school and home, I get to talk and play with my friends. Lots of times while talking my friend might ask me to pass the salt and pepper or take a turn on the video game. This is called following directions from friends.

Sometimes, my friend might ask me to do something like toss the ball. When he asks me to do something, it is important to think, "Is this okay? Is this safe?" Most of the time, the answer is "yes," and I can enjoy doing something for and with my friend. In this case, it would be okay to play ball.

If the answer is "no," I should think about what to do next. Sometimes, my friend might not know that it is not okay to do something at my house or my school. Like, if my friend asked me to jump off my couch onto the table and then jump to the floor like Spider-Man, I might have to tell them that, at my house, my mom doesn't like us to jump on furniture. But we could go outside and jump off a small rock. In this case, I needed to let my friend know that we couldn't jump on the furniture.

I think if I can try to ask myself these two questions: "Is this okay?" and "Is this safe?" it will help me think if I should follow the direction or not. When my friend asks me something, I can try and make a good decision about whether or not to follow my friend's direction.

Follow up the Social Story™ by asking children, "So, should you *always* follow someone else's direction?" If necessary, prompt the children to say "no," so that you can respond with "Tell me when it's important not to follow directions from friends." Prompt answers such as "When it is unsafe" and "When it is against some people's rules."

Lead a discussion about what to do when it is unsafe. Help the children create a consequence map that shows what might happen if they do something unsafe. Also, talk about the importance of thinking about different rules in different settings. For example, help the children make lists of rules for home and school and then compare and contrast these lists.

Use a cognitive behavioral intervention such as SODA. Help the children create a visual for Stop (S), Observe (O), Deliberate (D), Act (A).

    S   Stop and think (My friend is giving me directions.)

    O   Observe (Look around. What are others doing? What are others saying?)

    D   Deliberate (Should I be doing the same? Would it be safe to do so? What are the rules? What is my plan? What am I going to say and do?)

    A   Act (I have a plan. I am going to . . .)

Challenge for Step 6. Tell students you are going to give them a scenario and a T-chart. Their challenge is to list what is safe and what is not safe, what is following an important rule, and what is not following an important rule. Then, they should create a plan about what they think they would do. For example, tell students,

Nolan is visiting his friend's house. His mom left to go to the store to get some popcorn for the boys. She told them to stay inside. His friend asked Nolan to go in the backyard. What is expected? What is unexpected? What should Nolan do?

When each child has met the challenge, provide a celebration ceremony similar to the one in Step 6 of Skill #1.

Skill #3: Looking Where Others Are Looking

STEP 1

Play—Earning the First Puzzle Piece With I Spy

Framework Step	The Teacher Will:	The Children Will:
Step 1 **PLAY**	Teach the children to play the game that requires the use of the targeted social skill.	Use the targeted social skill in a fun and engaging game.

Use a modified version of the game I Spy to teach the skill of looking where others are looking. To set up the game:

1. Gather some big objects that are easy to describe and put them in places where they can be easily seen.
2. Appoint one person to be the player (the spy). (Optional: Get a pair of binoculars for the spy to use as a prop).

Directions for play. To play the game:

1. The spy looks through the binoculars, targets an object, and says, "I spy with my little eye . . . something that's green and little. Guess what I see!"
2. Players look in the direction the spy is looking toward to guess what the spy sees.

Variations. One variation on this game has the other children guess where the spy is looking without any descriptive words from the spy. For example, the spy says, "I spy something. Guess what I see?"

Teaching the game. For quick learners or experienced players, explain: "You are the players. Your goal is to guess what the spy is looking at. The best way to guess is to look where the spy is looking."

For early learners or new players, explain: "You are the players. Your goal is to guess where the spy is looking. Watch this . . ." Ask a colleague to hold up a large object. Look directly at the object and say, "I spy with my little eye . . . guess what I see!"

Now explain: "Your job is to look where I am looking. Let's practice. Watch me look at this!" (Look at colleague in far corner of the room with big object.) "Now, guess what I see!" Repeat this demonstration with the colleague going to four different parts of the room. Continue these demonstrations by looking at large objects around the room. Practice a few rounds individually and then start the game.

As they play the game, remind the children of the rules: "Look at the eyes of the spy when the spy says "I spy with my little eye . . . guess what I see!" Then, look where the spy is looking and guess what the spy sees."

Play the game many times, giving the children plenty of practice looking where the spy is looking. If necessary, let the spy give verbal cues, but as often as possible, let the children guess by looking where the spy is looking.

Challenge for Step 1. Give praise to students such as, "We've been playing the game I Spy and practicing looking where our friends are looking. You are doing great work!" Then follow up with the challenge: "I'll give you a Guess What I See chart with 10 spaces. You'll get a pirate sticker every time you correctly guess what the spy sees. When you get all 10, you will have earned your puzzle piece!" Each child should receive a token economy chart to fill in as they guess what the spy sees. When each child has met the challenge, provide a celebration ceremony similar to that in Step 1 of Skill #1.

STEP 2
Talk—Earning the Second Puzzle Piece

Framework Step	The Teacher Will:	The Children Will:
Step 2 **TALK**	Teach the children to name the social skill and say when it should be used.	Name the skill and, given a hypothetical situation, tell when it should be used.

Start a discussion about the skill of looking where others are looking: "Remember when we played I Spy? What happened in that game?" If necessary, shape answers such as, "We guessed what the spy was looking at" or "We looked where the spy was looking."

Then, ask children, "And, how did you know what the spy was seeing?" If necessary, shape answers such as, "We looked at the spy's eyes" or "We looked where the spy turned his head."

Explain to the children that this skill is called "looking where someone is looking." Then, ask children, "When might you need to look at where someone is looking?" If necessary, shape answers such as:

- To see what they see.
- To help them get what they want.
- To think about what they are thinking.

What do we call it when you watch someone's eyes and guess what they see?	When might you want to look where others are looking?
	1.
	2.
	3.
	4.
	5.

Figure 38. Activity sheet for Skill #3.

- To see what they might need.

Challenge for Step 2. Tell students you have a challenge for them: "You will be able to answer the following questions and complete the activity sheet with a friend. When you have answered these questions, bring it to me. When everyone has five good answers, we'll present puzzle piece #2." Give each child a copy of the activity sheet in Figure 38. When each child has met the challenge, provide a celebration ceremony similar to the one in Step 2 of Skill #1.

STEP 3

Act—Earning the Third Puzzle Piece

Framework Step	The Teacher Will:	The Children Will:
Step 3 ACT	Teach the children to demonstrate the skill in an engineered situation.	Act out the skill in a role-playing or engineered situation.

Set up role-playing situations to help children reinforce the concept of looking where others are looking such as these:

Role-play 1: Something neat and new
Actor: *Walks into room.* "Oh, wow!"
Audience: *Looks to see what Actor 1 sees, then makes similar comments.*
"Wow. Awesome. Cool. Neat."

Role-play 2: Something broken
Actor: *Walks into room.* "Oh, no!"
Audience: *Looks to see what Actor 1 sees, then makes similar comments.*
"Ooh, that's sad. Oh, how bad. Aww."

Role-play 3: Something unexpected or scary
Actor: *Walks into room.* "Yikes!"
Audience: *Looks to see what Actor 1 sees, then makes similar comments.*
"Ooh, that's scary. Ouch, that must have hurt!"

Create opportunities that require joint attention. For example, set up a puzzle, giving each child control of half of the pieces. Another idea is to set up a turn-taking procedure where one child starts a drawing and the others take turns adding to it. Also, play with games or toys that do unexpected things (such as pop up or crash). Provide a model of looking at the children when such things happen, and encourage them to look at each other. Special activities such as art projects, having visitors, and taking walks can create opportunities to encourage children to look where others are looking.

Challenge for Step 3. Tell students,

We've been looking where others are looking and guess what? It's time for your challenge! You'll get to select one activity from the choice board and take five turns with a friend. When you are working on a cooperative task, be sure to watch what your friend is doing. The best way to do that will be to look where your friend is looking!

Give each child the choice board in Figure 39. When each child has met the challenge, provide a celebration ceremony similar to the one in Step 3 of Skill #1.

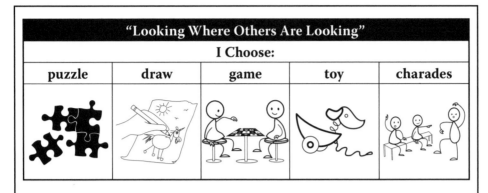

Figure 39. Choice board for Skill #3.

STEP 4

Use—Earning the Fourth Puzzle Piece

Framework Step		The Teacher Will:	The Children Will:
Step 4 **USE**		Teach the children to use the skill in natural settings.	Use the skill with others in a school or home setting.

To help children generalize their skill of "looking where others are looking," create opportunities for them to do this in the natural environment. For example, put a big package of chips up on the shelf. Look at the food and say something like, "It's time for snack. What should we have?" Wait for the children to follow your gaze. Then, respond by saying, "Wow, let's have chips!" Or as you take walks, look at different things and wait for children to shift their gaze to where you are looking. When necessary, make comments that catch their attention. Use natural gestures to shape gaze shifting and remember that explicit instruction may be necessary for some children to learn to follow the direction of a pointing finger.

To check for eye contact and gaze shifting, do something sudden such as turning on the TV, a computer, a tape recorder, an iPod, or the radio. If necessary, prompt children to look where others are looking and reinforce with natural consequences such as comments and opportunities to watch or listen to what just came on.

Teaching simple magic tricks to children is a wonderful way to get them to look where others are looking. The magic wand acts as a natural cue to look at the tricks. Magic tricks provide unexpected results that children can hardly resist watching.

Challenge for Step 4. Praise students by saying, "Wow! What a great job you have done looking where others are looking!" Then give them the challenge:

> I'm going to watch you read a book with a friend. I'll be watching to see if you are looking at the same pictures as your friend. I'm going to keep a secret chart and we'll look at it when you have finished looking at the book together. If I make 10 marks on your chart, you'll earn your puzzle piece!

When each child has met the challenge, provide a celebration ceremony similar to the one in Step 4 of Skill #1.

STEP 5

Explain—Earning the Fifth Puzzle Piece

Framework Step	The Teacher Will:	The Children Will:
Step 5 **EXPLAIN**	Teach the children the rationale for using the skill.	Say why the skill is effective in interacting with others.

Use Social Thinking® strategies to guide a discussion, explaining that other people have thoughts. Tell children that they can sometimes guess what other people are thinking about if they know where they are looking. Provide other reasons the skill might be useful. Summarize the discussion by asking, "Why is it good to look where someone is looking?" If necessary, prompt answers such as:

- You might want to know what they are seeing.
- You might see something you can do to help someone.
- You might see something fun to talk about.
- You might get an idea of what the person is thinking about.

Follow up by telling children, "It's good to look where someone is looking when you are working on a project together. For example:

- You might know if the person is waiting for you to take a turn.
- You can see if the person is looking and working and know to wait a minute.
- You might be able to tell if it's a good time to share an idea with that person.

■ You might see that the person is busy, and it's not a good time to interrupt."

Pose questions to get students thinking about the consequences of not using the skill:

■ What can happen if someone is walking down the hall and not watching?
■ What can happen if someone crosses the street without looking?
■ What can happen if someone is looking down while walking in the cafeteria?
■ What can happen if someone is looking down at the floor while walking in a store?

After children have discussed these scenarios, remind them of the importance of the skill by saying, "When you show something to someone and you want to talk about it, you should check to see if they are looking. If they are not looking, they might not be interested in talking about your topic." Direct a discussion on how to know if someone is interested in a topic. Help children use a graphic organizer like the one in Figure 40 to record their thoughts.

Challenge for Step 5. This step includes two possible challenges. For the first challenge, tell students,

All day long, I will be pretending not to look where I am going. If you catch me, let me know, and I will put a star on your chart. When you have three stars, you'll earn your puzzle piece for Step 5.

For the second challenge, tell students,

Come and share something with me. Watch to see if I am looking at you and looking at what you are sharing. If I am, keep talking. If I am not, tell me and I will put a star on your chart. When you have three stars, you'll earn your puzzle piece for Step 5.

When each child has met a challenge, provide a celebration ceremony similar to the one in Step 5 of Skill #1.

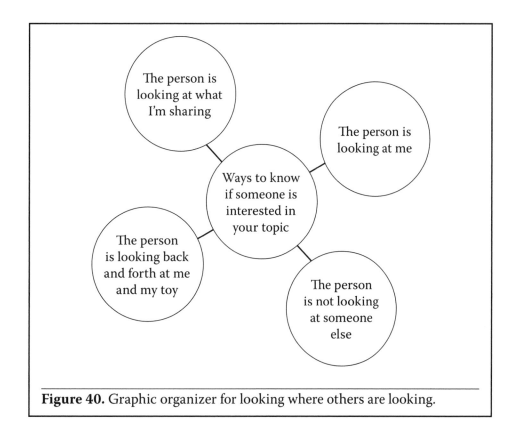

Figure 40. Graphic organizer for looking where others are looking.

STEP 6

Adjust—Earning the Sixth Puzzle Piece

Framework Step	The Teacher Will:	The Children Will:
Step 6 ADJUST	Teach the children to use flexible thinking and problem solving.	List and demonstrate an alternative action whenever the social skill is not effective.

Ask children, "Why is it good to look where someone is looking?" If necessary, shape answers such as:

- You might want to know what they are seeing.
- You might see something fun to talk about.
- You might see something you can do to help someone.
- You might be able to figure out what the person is thinking about.

Reinforce this by telling the children, "Yes, it's good to look where someone is looking. What happens if you can't tell where someone is looking?" If necessary, prompt such answers as:

- You could look at their eyes.
- You could look at things around the person.
- You could look at the eyes of others.
- You could ask.

Explain that it's important to know if a person is looking at you or not. Use a Social Story™ or power card to reinforce your instruction (see Figures 41 and 42). Explain to students:

When you're talking to someone, it's good to know if that person is looking at you or not. If someone looks at you while you are talking, that person may be interested in what you are saying. That means you might be able to talk a little more. If the person is not looking at you, it's possible that the person does not want to listen to you talk about that topic anymore. Then, you could wait a few seconds to see if the person asks you a question. If not, you could ask a question, such as, "What do you think?"

Challenge for Step 6. Tell students they are going to have a Show and Tell presentation the next day and their job is to bring something to show the class and prepare some things to say about what they are showing. Explain, "When you are talking, watch the eyes of other people. If they are looking at you, you might say a little more. If they are looking away, you might pause and see if anyone has a question." Students who look where others are looking will earn a puzzle piece for this step.

An easy way to measure this is to make a video of the presentations, then gauge whether students were looking where others are looking and making good decisions about whether to talk more or let others have a turn. When each child has met the challenge, provide a celebration similar to the one in Step 6 of Skill #1.

Power Card: "Superman Uses His Eyes"

Superman uses his eyes to watch people. He looks at their eyes to tell where they are looking. When they are looking at him, he talks a little more. When they are not looking, he stops to see if they have something to say. If they don't say anything, he asks a question.

Superman would be proud if he knew you were trying to:

1. Watch the eyes of others to see if you should keep talking.
2. Talk a little more when people are looking at you.
3. Wait to see what they have to say when they are not looking at you.
4. Ask a question if no one says anything.

Figure 41. Power card.

Social Story™ for Looking Where Others Are Looking

When we talk to other people, it's important to check where they are looking. Because people are usually thinking about what they are looking at, we might be able to guess what they are thinking about by looking where they are looking.

This is especially important in Show and Tell. If my friends are looking at me, they are probably interested in what I am saying. Then, I can talk a little more. If my friends are not looking at me, I might be talking too much or talking too fast or talking too loudly.

If that is happening, it might be time for me to stop talking and wait for someone else to have a turn. If no one else talks, then it might be a good time for me to ask a question. When I'm sharing things in Show and Tell, I will try to look where others are looking.

Figure 42. Social story.

Skill #4: Asking Questions

Play—Earning the First Puzzle Piece With Twenty Questions

Framework Step	The Teacher Will:	The Children Will:
Step 1 **PLAY**	Teach the children to play the game that requires the use of the targeted social skill.	Use the targeted social skill in a fun and engaging game.

Use the game Twenty Questions to teach the skill of asking questions for information. To set up the game, give one child at the front of the room an object in a paper bag.

Directions for play. To play the game:

1. The player peeks in the bag to see the object.
2. Audience members take turns asking questions about the object.
3. The questions must be able to be answered with "yes" or "no."
4. The player wins if it takes more than 20 questions to guess the object.
5. The audience wins if it takes less than 20 questions to guess.

Variations.

- Children can write down the name of something they are thinking about.
- Children can work in pairs and then change roles with their partners.
- Set up the game so that children can ask who, what, when, where, and why questions.

Teaching the game. For quick learners or experienced players, explain:

When it's your turn, look into your bag at the object. Don't show it to anyone else. Everyone else in the audience will ask you questions about your object. If you know the answer, say it. If you don't know, you can say, "I don't know."

When you are in the audience, you should ask questions that will help you guess the name of the object in the bag. However, the player can only answer "yes" or "no." So, you can't ask, "What's in the bag?" You have to ask questions like, "Is it blue?" or "Can you play with it?"

☐ Question 1	☐ Question 6	☐ Question 11	☐ Question 16
☐ Question 2	☐ Question 7	☐ Question 12	☐ Question 17
☐ Question 3	☐ Question 8	☐ Question 13	☐ Question 18
☐ Question 4	☐ Question 9	☐ Question 14	☐ Question 19
☐ Question 5	☐ Question 10	☐ Question 15	☐ Question 20

Figure 43. Chart for recording how many questions are asked.

For early learners or new players, explain: "You are the players. Your goal is to guess what I have in this bag. Watch this." Demonstrate how to play by peeking in the bag and having your colleague ask you some "yes" or "no" questions.

Practice a few rounds, letting children ask questions and then start the game. Remind the children of the rules: "Remember to ask questions that can be answered with 'yes' or 'no.' Use your knowledge of features and functions and categories to help you ask questions."

Once the children are comfortable playing the game, increase the difficulty by bringing in less common objects. Then, set up the game so that children can ask who, what, when, where, and why questions. You can use the chart in Figure 43 to help facilitate the playing of this game.

Challenge for Step 1. Give students the challenge of playing Twenty Questions by themselves while you watch. Tell them, "For this game, you'll work with a partner to try to guess what's in the bag by asking questions. When you have asked 20 questions, you'll have met your challenge!" When each child has met the challenge, provide a celebration ceremony similar to the one described in Step 1 of Skill #1.

STEP 2
Talk—Earning the Second Puzzle Piece

Framework Step	The Teacher Will:	The Children Will:
Step 2 TALK	Teach the children to name the social skill and say when it should be used.	Name the skill and, given a hypothetical situation, tell when it should be used.

Start a discussion about the skill of getting another person's attention: "Remember when we played Twenty Questions? What happened in that game?" Prompt answers such as:

- We had a secret in the bag.
- We solved the mystery.
- We asked questions.
- We listened to the answers to our questions.

Use Direct Instruction such as the following to teach about the skill:

Teacher: This skill is called asking questions. When you don't know something, it's good to ask questions. What's the skill?

Children: Asking questions.

Teacher: Great! When can you use it?

Children: When you don't know something.

Teacher: Terrific!

Now, use a graphic organizer to brainstorm answers to this question, "When are some other times that you need to ask questions?" Guide students to provide answers with the five w's and an h questions, such as "When you want to know what something is or "when you want to know where something is."

Challenge for Step 2. Tell students,

All week long, you'll need to be ready for me to ask you questions about this social skill! I'll be keeping track of the answers you give me and, when you have 10 good answers, you'll have met this challenge. I'll ask you questions such as:

1. We've been working on a social skill, and I have a challenge for you! We played a game, and one person had a bag with a secret in it. You used a social skill to find out what was in that bag. Your challenge is to name that social skill!
2. If you want to know how to do something, what could you do? (Ask questions.)
3. When might it be important to ask questions? (When you want to know where something is or when it will be time to go.)

When each child has met the challenge, provide a celebration ceremony similar to the one in Step 2 of Skill #1.

STEP 3

Act—Earning the Third Puzzle Piece

Framework Step	The Teacher Will:	The Children Will:
Step 3 **ACT**	Teach the children to demonstrate the skill in an engineered situation.	Act out the skill in a role-playing or engineered situation.

Praise students by saying, "You have been doing so well with our new social skill!" Set up the role-plays for Step 3 by telling students, "I will give you some scripts. You'll be the actors and you'll get to ask and answer lots of questions!" Set up role-playing situations like the following:

Actor 1: *Mom is getting her purse and keys.*
Actor 2: Where are we going? What are we going to do there?

Actor 1: *Playing with a new toy.*
Actor 2: What is that? How does it work?

Actor 1: *Watching TV.*
Actor 2: What are you watching? What's it about?

Actor 1: *Teacher gives instructions.* Okay, let's get started!
Actor 2: *Raises hand.* Can I ask a question!

Practice scenes such as the ones above, switching roles among the children. If possible, take pictures and review the pictures, or make a video and watch them as movies. To enhance the experience, add titles to the videos such as "Asking Questions! Starring Robby and Doug."

Coach the children to use various ways of asking questions and ask them for their ideas for role-plays. Provide modeling to help them add appropriate intonation and body language into their actions. Some prompts for role-plays might include:

- "Want to play a little ball?"
- "What's your favorite TV show?"
- "Could you help me, please?"

Challenge for Step 3. Tell students,

Okay, we've been working on a social skill, and I have a challenge for you! I am going to set up the movie camera to see if I can get you in a video using your new social skill. I'll be bringing in a big box, and we'll see what you do! When we watch the video, if you have asked a question, you'll have met your challenge!

The goal is for students to ask you about what's in the box. When each child has met the challenge, provide a celebration ceremony similar to the one in Step 3 of Skill #1.

STEP 4
Use—Earning the Fourth Puzzle Piece

Framework Step	The Teacher Will:	The Children Will:
Step 4 **USE**	Teach the children to use the skill in natural settings.	Use the skill with others in a school or home setting.

Use activity-based instruction and incidental teaching techniques to set up some situations to see if the children will use the skill in a more natural situation. For example, bring in a big box with something like a trumpet inside. Wait a few minutes to see if they ask you any questions like: "What's in the box?" or "Who is that for?" Ask a colleague (or one child) to peek into the box and wait. Reward naturally occurring questions with information and comments. If necessary, prompt questions until everyone knows what's in the box. Then, model or prompt questions such as, "Can I have a turn?" and, "What does that sound like?" "How do you think we can make it sound different?" "Do you know anyone who plays the trumpet?" "Have you ever seen one of these before?" "Where?"

Set up a token economy to keep track of the number of questions children ask others. When possible, transfer this tracking method to the children themselves so that they are engaged in self-monitoring.

Challenge for Step 4. Tell students,

This week, we've been talking about asking questions. You each have a different challenge this week, but each of you will have a chart to keep up with your questions. We'll do this during recess and lunchtime for 3 days.

Give each child a set number of questions to be asked. When each child has met the challenge, provide a celebration ceremony similar to the one in Step 4 of Skill #1.

STEP 5
Explain—Earning the Fifth Puzzle Piece

Framework Step	The Teacher Will:	The Children Will:
Step 5 EXPLAIN	Teach the children the rationale for using the skill.	Say why the skill is effective in interacting with others.

Use a Social Story™ such as the one below to help children learn reasons for asking questions.

Why It's Important to Ask Questions?
     When people talk to each other, they sometimes ask questions. The first reason that people ask questions is to show that they are interested in other people. For example, when they see friends at school, they might ask, "Hi! How are you?" The second reason they ask questions is to learn things about people. For instance, they could ask "Do you like LEGOs™? When they want to follow up, they can ask a question like, "What are your favorite LEGO™ sets?" The third reason they might ask questions is to start conversations with people. For instance, they might ask, "Have you seen any movies, lately?" The fourth reason they ask questions is to get to do something together. For example, they might ask, "Do you want to play?" or "Will you help me?"
     I will try to ask questions because it might show that I am interested in people. Asking questions might help me show that I am interested in others. They might also help me learn about others, start conversations, or do something with other people.

Use a graphic organizer to help the children brainstorm ideas for why it is important to ask questions. To guide the brainstorming, ask children the following questions:
- Why is it good to ask questions?
- How does asking questions help you make friends?
- When does asking questions interfere with getting along with others?
- How can you tell if you might be asking too many questions?
- How can you tell if you ask a question that might bother someone?

Challenge for Step 5. Tell students,

Your challenge is to be able to answer some questions about asking questions! All week long, I'll be stopping you to ask you some questions such as: Why is it good to ask questions? I'll keep track on my chart and when you have 10 answers that are thoughtful and appropriate, you'll earn puzzle piece #5!

When each child has met the challenge, provide a celebration ceremony similar to the one described in Step 5 of Skill #1.

STEP 6

Adjust—Earning the Sixth Puzzle Piece

Framework Step	The Teacher Will:	The Children Will:
Step 6 ADJUST	Teach the children to use flexible thinking and problem solving.	List and demonstrate an alternative action whenever the social skill is not effective.

Use Direct Instruction to teach children to think flexibly. Tell the children that it is important to ask:

- appropriate questions,
- at an appropriate time,
- to an appropriate person, and
- in an appropriate situation.

Use Cognitive Behavior Modification techniques to help children think through these questions:

- Is it a good question? (Do I really want or need to know the answer?)
- Is this the right person to ask? (Is this person likely to know and give me the best answer?
- Is this a good time to ask? (Is the person busy with something else?)
- Is this a good place to ask? (Can we talk here or is the question related to the place?)
- Is this a good way to ask? (With polite words and a questioning tone?)

Use cartooning to help children learn what other people might be thinking if they ask too many questions or ask a question that might make others feel uncomfortable.

For the skill of questioning, the goal may be, for some children, to increase their ability and comfort levels in asking questions. For others, it may be to help them discriminate between good times to ask questions and bad times to ask questions. For still others, it may be appropriate to limit the number of questions they ask others and to teach them ways of finding out information on their own.

Use consequence maps to help children organize information such as:

- The consequences of asking too many questions:
  » It gets annoying.
  » People get mad.
  » People think you are weird.
  » People might avoid you.

- How you might know if you asked too many questions:
  » People might walk away.
  » People look surprised or mad.
  » People stop answering.
  » People answer only in one word.

- What to do if you asked too many questions:
  » Stop and listen for a while.
  » Stop and think about what the other person might be thinking.
  » Apologize, saying something like, "Gosh, I'm asking too many questions. Let's talk about something else."

- What you might do if you asked a question that embarrassed someone:
  » Apologize, saying something like, "Gosh, I'm sorry if I offended you."
  » Apologize, saying something like, "I'm sorry—that wasn't a good thing to ask. Let's talk about something else."

Challenge for Step 6. Tell students,

You've been doing so well with asking questions! I'm just amazed at all you've learned! Here's your challenge. Come up with three possible questions for one (or more) of the following situations:

1. You meet a friend at the mall and you want to start a conversation.
2. You are playing on the playground and you want someone to play ball with you.
3. You have a new computer game and you want help learning how to play it.

4. You go to a birthday party and see someone you don't know and you want to talk.
5. You go over to a friend's house to play and you want to play a game.

When each child has met the challenge, provide a celebration ceremony similar to the one in Step 6 of Skill #1.

Skill #5: Sharing Things With Others

STEP 1

Play—Earning the First Puzzle Piece With Give Away Lotto

Framework Step	The Teacher Will:	The Children Will:
Step 1 PLAY	Teach the children to play the game that requires the use of the targeted social skill.	Use the targeted social skill in a fun and engaging game.

Use the game Give Away Lotto to teach the skill of sharing things with others. To set up the game:
1. Give each child a Lotto card (see game 1 for ideas for Lotto cards).
2. Give the children some of the matching pieces for each card except their own.

Directions for play. To play the game:
1. Direct children to look at the boards of other children.
2. Instruct them to look at their own pieces and offer them to the children who need them.
3. Tell them to take turns giving matching pieces to their friends until at least one board is covered with chips.
4. When all of the pictures are gone, the winner yells, "I've shared all my pieces!"

Variations.
- Boards of 4 to 25 can be created depending on the level of the children.
- Lotto cards can be pictures, letters, numbers, words, symbols, or signs.
- Pieces can be exact matches or can be written words.

- Start with pictures children are happy to give away. That is, at first, they don't need to give away their favorite pieces.

Teaching the game. For quick learners or experienced players, explain:

You are the players. Your goal is to give away all your pieces. The first one to give everything away is the winner. Start by looking at the boards of your friends. You have the matching pieces for their boards. So, when it's your turn, call one friend by name and offer him or her a matching piece by saying something like, "Hey Max, would you like a basketball?" When someone asks you, you should say something like, "Sure! Thanks!" or "Yes, I would like a basketball!"

For early learners or new players, explain: "You are the players. Your goal is to give away all your pieces. Watch this . . ." Demonstrate play by looking at the board of one child and saying something like, "Corey has a transportation board and I have a picture of a helicopter. So, I'll say this, 'Corey, would you like a helicopter?'"

Now explain: "So, let's practice. We'll each take a turn to look at the boards of our friends."

Again, demonstrate for the children:

Jessica, look at Corey's board. What kinds of pictures does Corey have? Right! Corey has transportation pieces! What picture do you have that Corey needs? Terrific! Corey does need a train picture, so, now say, "Corey, would you like a train?"

Practice a few rounds individually and then start the game. Remind the children of the rules: "Your job is to give away your pieces. Keep looking at the boards of your friends so you can ask them if they want your pieces." Play the game many times, giving the children plenty of opportunities to share.

Challenge for Step 1. Praise students for their work, then tell them they will be playing the game one more time. Explain: "I will be looking for students who look at their friends' pieces and then share three of your pieces with three friends without any help. Let's see if you can remember how to play. Ready, let's play!" When each child has met the challenge, provide a celebration ceremony similar to the one in Step 1 of Skill #1.

STEP 2

Talk—Earning the Second Puzzle Piece

Framework Step	The Teacher Will:	The Children Will:
Step 2 **TALK**	Teach the children to name the social skill and say when it should be used.	Name the skill and, given a hypothetical situation, tell when it should be used.

Start a discussion about the skill of sharing: "Remember when we played Give Away Lotto? What happened in that game?" If necessary, shape answers such as, "We gave away our pictures" and "We shared our pictures."

Use Direct Instruction to teach the answer ("sharing with others") when you ask, "What is it called when you . . .

- let someone use your toy?
- give away some of your snack?
- let someone take a turn with something you're playing with?"

To develop further understanding, use Discrete Trial Training to teach children to recognize when to use the skill.

- You have lots of snack, and your friend doesn't have any. What could you do?
- You have a blue marker, and your friend wants to use it. What could you do?
- You have a new toy, and your friends are excited about it. What could you do?

Challenge for Step 2. Tell students,

We've been talking about the skill called "sharing with others." This means that you might offer someone else a turn with something or the item itself. Now, this is your challenge: Throughout the day, I am going to ask you the name of our new social skill and questions about when to use it. I'll keep track on a chart and when you have 10 great answers, you'll have met your challenge!

Throughout the day, pose situations to the children such as:

- Elena looked in her bag and saw that her mom sent her favorite Disney characters. Elena knew that Josiah loved Mickey Mouse, so what should Elena do?

- Jasmine and Julie were at the sandbox. Jasmine was shoveling sand into a bucket. Julie didn't have a shovel. What should Jasmine do?

When each child has met the challenge, provide a celebration ceremony similar to the one in Step 2 of Skill #1.

STEP 3

Act—Earning the Third Puzzle Piece

Framework Step		The Teacher Will:	The Children Will:
Step 3 ACT		Teach the children to demonstrate the skill in an engineered situation.	Act out the skill in a role-playing or engineered situation.

Set up role-playing situations that require children to share with others. Use situations such as these:

Actor 1: *Is playing with all of the blocks.*
Actor 2: *Walks over to carpet and sits down.*
Actor 1: Do you want some blocks?

Actor 1: *Is eating chips.*
Actor 2: *Walks over to table and sits down.*
Actor 1: Do you want some chips?

Actor 1: *Is playing a computer game.*
Actor 2: *Walks over to computer.*
Actor 1: Do you want a turn on the computer?

Use activity-based instruction to create opportunities throughout the day to practice sharing. For example, set up materials for an art activity. Give out materials so that one child has all the crayons, one has all the glue, another has all the scissors. Make sure there are fewer items than needed so children will need to share. Or, share computer time activity with pairs of children. The children share the time allotted on the computer. Some children might benefit from a visual schedule to show when their turn begins and ends.

Challenge for Step 3. Tell students,

Okay, we have been practicing sharing with our friends. Your next challenge is to go to your center stations. You will have three stations to work in with a friend. I will be watching. Each time I see you sharing, I will walk over and give you a high five. When you have received three high fives from me, you will have earned puzzle piece #3!

When each child has met the challenge, provide a celebration ceremony similar to the one in Step 3 of Skill #1.

STEP 4

Use—Earning the Fourth Puzzle Piece

Framework Step	The Teacher Will:	The Children Will:
Step 4 **USE**	Teach the children to use the skill in natural settings.	Use the skill with others in a school or home setting.

Continue to provide opportunities for the children to practice in the natural environment and reinforce efforts with a token economy. You can also use an Incredible 5-Point Scale (see Figure 44) to provide feedback for children on how they are performing when sharing. Provide reinforcement when children are on the top level. Some children may need shaping, so for those, provide reinforcement as they are making progress in moving toward the top level.

Pair students with peers in a variety of activities throughout the day and embed activities that promote sharing. For instance, provide one child with the items needed to create a project (glue and paper). Provide the other child with pictures of favorite characters or other items to use. The arrangement of the materials naturally provides the opportunity to share.

Challenge for Step 4. Using a token economy, explain to students,

We have been practicing sharing with our friends. This week, I am going to see how fast you can fill up your chart. There are 10 spaces for sharing on your chart. I'll put a sticker there every time I see you share with someone. When your chart is completed, you will have earned your fourth puzzle piece! Let's work on being a good friend and sharing.

When each child has met the challenge, provide a celebration ceremony similar to the one in Step 4 of Skill #1.

	I played with the toy a little of the time and I shared a lot.
	I played with the toy some of the time, but I shared quite a bit.
	I played with the toy some but I shared some.
	I played with the toy all the time, but I shared a little.
	I played with the toy all the time and did not share at all.

Figure 44. Incredible 5-Point Scale for skill #5.

STEP 5
Explain—Earning the Fifth Puzzle Piece

Framework Step	The Teacher Will:	The Children Will:
Step 5 EXPLAIN	Teach the children the rationale for using the skill.	Say why the skill is effective in interacting with others.

In this discussion, use the principles of Social Thinking® to help the children think about why it is important to share with others. Say something like, "Friends, we have had lots of fun sharing. Can anyone tell me why this might be important?" Shape answers such as:

- If I share, then someone might share with me.
- It makes me happy to get things from others, so I should do the same.
- If I don't share, then no one will share with me.

Then tell students, "Great, it does sound like we know that sharing is important. What happens when you are sharing with others?" Prompt answers such as:

- I get to see something or play with something I like.
- My friend gets to see something that I give them, then I get to see it.
- It makes my friend feel good.
- It makes me feel good.

Use a power card to help children remember to share. Consider putting a picture of a celebrity or favorite character on the card as a reminder to students. For example, a picture of Taylor Swift might say, "Taylor Swift shares her music with the entire world."

Challenge for Step 5. Praise students by saying, "What magnificent friends you have been this week!" Then, give them their challenge:

> I want you to create your own story that tells about the skill of sharing and why it is important. In the story, be sure to tell the good things that might happen when you share with others. And, include some things that might happen when you don't share. When your stories are complete, we'll read them aloud to the class. If your story explains the importance of sharing, you'll earn puzzle piece #5!

Before reading the stories aloud, check to see that they are all appropriate. If necessary, provide feedback to shape the child's thinking and help the child revise the story. Once the stories are completed, review them with the children to make sure each child can explain why the social skill is important. When each child has met the challenge, provide a celebration ceremony similar to the one in Step 5 of Skill #1.

STEP 6

Adjust—Earning the Sixth Puzzle Piece

Framework Step	The Teacher Will:	The Children Will:
Step 6 ADJUST	Teach the children to use flexible thinking and problem solving.	List and demonstrate an alternative action whenever the social skill is not effective.

Explain to the children that having good social skills means being able to think about whether or not to do something. Remind them that this skill was about sharing and that it's usually good to share. Ask them, "What are some things that you should share?"

Then say, "Now, think about this! What are some things that you should not share?" Use a graphic organizer to help the children brainstorm ideas of things that they should not share. Then, have the children create a cue card to post in the room (see Figure 45) of items or activities that are appropriate to share with friends and those that they should not consider sharing. After creating the cue

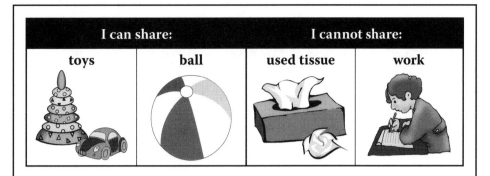

Figure 45. Cue card of items appropriate and inappropriate for sharing.

card, start a discussion like this: "I see that you can share toys and the ball. Why can you not share a tissue or your work?" Prompt answers such as:

- A tissue that I have used is only for me.
- It is not healthy to share my tissue.
- Sometimes, my teacher only wants to see what I can do.
- When we are working on a test, I cannot share my answers.

Continue with this discussion by asking, "Is there a time that you could share tissues?" Shape such answers such as:

- You could hand someone the box of new tissues.
- You could hand someone a tissue that has not been used.

Follow through by asking, "Great, might there be a time when you can share your work?" Prompt answers such as:

- When my teacher says we can work together.
- When my teacher says show your work to a friend.

Challenge for Step 6. Reinforce the students by first saying, "You are turning into super flexible thinkers! I can tell that you know that sometimes it's good to share and sometimes it's not." Then set up the challenge activity:

I have index cards for each of you. Several times over the next few days, I will stop and let you fill out one of these cards. You'll need to think about whether or not you shared during that time. Then, mark one of the choices in the top box. Write down what you shared or what you didn't share. Then answer the questions. When you have five cards that you are proud to show me, turn them into me. We'll review them and if we agree that you have made good choices, you'll have earned puzzle piece #5!

Thinking About Sharing		
Mark one of these and then answer the questions below.		
❑ I shared: _____		
❑ I did not share: _____		
Was this something that was safe or healthy to share?	❑ Yes	❑ No
Was it the right time to share?	❑ Yes	❑ No
If needed, did I have permission from an adult to share?	❑ Yes	❑ No
Overall, did I make the right choice?	❑ Yes	❑ No

Figure 46. Challenge card for Step 6 of Skill #5.

Give each student the card in Figure 46. When each child has met the challenge, provide a celebration ceremony similar to the one in Step 6 of Skill #1.

Skill #6: Making Appropriate Comments During Competitive Activities

STEP 1

Play—Earning the First Puzzle Piece With Rock, Paper, Scissors

Framework Step	The Teacher Will:	The Children Will:
Step 1 **PLAY**	Teach the children to play the game that requires the use of the targeted social skill.	Use the targeted social skill in a fun and engaging game.

Use the game Rock, Paper, Scissors to teach the skill of making appropriate comments about winning and losing during competitive activities. Because this game came can be played quickly and repeated many times in a row, it provides multiple opportunities for a child to practice this skill. Consider using a visual

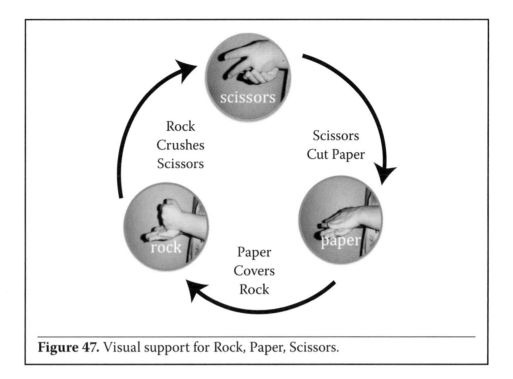

Figure 47. Visual support for Rock, Paper, Scissors.

support (such as the one in Figure 47) to display the hand movements and what each gesture represents in the course of the game.

Teaching the game. Tell the children that they are going to learn to play the game Rock, Paper, Scissors. Explain to them that this game is played very quickly and is usually played several times in a row, at least three. Tell the children that it is a game that they will play with their hands.

Show the visual support to the children. Demonstrate and explain that "rock" is symbolized by a closed, clenched fist; "paper" is represented by a flat hand facing downward with the fingers touching; and "scissors" is demonstrated by extending and separating the index and middle fingers only. Provide demonstrations of the gestures for the players.

Use Discrete Trial Training to teach the hand movements to the children. Provide several opportunities for the children to demonstrate each of the three gestures, initially focusing on one at a time. Call out the name of the gesture, (i.e., "show me rock"), allow 3–5 seconds for the response, and provide praise and descriptive feedback to the children. Continue this until all children can demonstrate all three gestures proficiently.

Explain that each gesture wins over one of the other gestures. Use the visual support to show the following: rock crushes scissors, scissors cut paper, and paper covers rock. Tell children that it is a tie when both players throw the same gesture during the same game. The goal is to select a gesture that defeats the opponent's gesture. Role-play the outcomes of the different gestures with the players.

Figure 48. Appropriate comments choice board.

Finally, tell the children that each game is played with two players. Explain that each player should make a fist like the rock symbol and touch that fist to the palm of the other hand while saying, "Rock, Paper, Scissors, *go!*" Once they say "go," at the same time, both players throw a gesture.

Play a few practice games with the children and model appropriate comments for winning and losing. Consider using a visual prompt such as a choice board (see Figure 48) of comments that the children can refer to as they are learning the skill.

Provide positive reinforcement in the form of descriptive praise statements to the children throughout the game. Set up a token economy for each child. Arrange for each child to work toward earning 10 tokens for making appropriate comments about winning and losing while playing the game.

Use descriptive praise statements during the game such as:
- "Alex, give yourself a check! I like how you told Eric 'Good game!'"
- "Erin, you're 2 checks away from earning your 10! Keep up the great work!"
- "Rodrick, you're a great sport! I saw you give Olivia a high five when she won the last time. Give yourself a check!"

Challenge for Step 1. First, praise students for their comments: "Everyone has done a super job of playing the game Rock, Paper, Scissors and making appropriate comments whether you win or lose. Way to go!" Then, give students the challenge for the first puzzle piece:

I am going to give you each a point card with five boxes. I'm going to pair you up with a new partner. You two will play the game and you'll each put a star in your box when you make an acceptable comment during the game. When you have five stars, you've met the challenge!

When each child has met the challenge, provide a celebration ceremony similar to the one in Step 1 of Skill #1.

STEP 2
Talk—Earning the Second Puzzle Piece

Framework Step	The Teacher Will:	The Children Will:
Step 2 **TALK**	Teach the children to name the social skill and say when it should be used.	Name the skill and, given a hypothetical situation, tell when it should be used.

Use Discrete Trial Training to teach the children to name the skill in many different situations. For example, say, "Do you remember the game, Rock, Paper, Scissors? After each game, we said things like, 'You won! Congratulations!' or 'Rats, I lost!' We call this making appropriate comments during competitions."
Ask questions such as:
- If you win, what could you say? (Yes!)
- What's the skill called? (Making appropriate comments about winning.)
- If you lose, what could you say? (Rats, I lost!)
- What's the skill called? (Making appropriate comments about losing.)
- When are some other times that you could make comments like this?
  - » When your favorite team wins or loses.
  - » When somebody makes a good grade.
  - » When somebody wins a spelling bee.

Create a graphic organizer to help children make lists of additional things that they can say and other times they could use the skill. (See the challenge below for an example.) Use the graphic organizer for group instruction while teaching and for individuals during the challenge.
Challenge for Step 2. Tell students,

Everyone has done a nice job of telling me the name of our new skill and talking about when you would need to use this skill. The challenge for earning puzzle piece #2 is to fill out the graphic organizer (see Figure

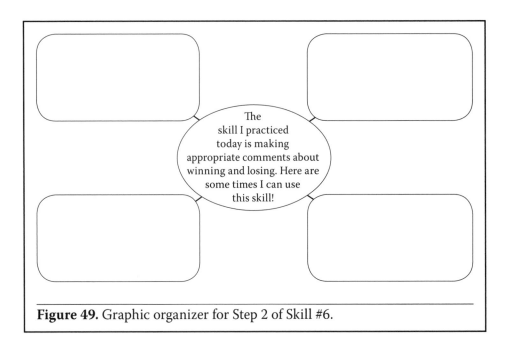

Figure 49. Graphic organizer for Step 2 of Skill #6.

49) that I am going to give you. After all of the charts are complete, we will share the information written and have a celebration.

When each child has met the challenge, provide a celebration ceremony similar to the one in Step 2 of Skill #1.

STEP 3
Act—Earning the Third Puzzle Piece

Framework Step	The Teacher Will:	The Children Will:
Step 3 ACT	Teach the children to demonstrate the skill in an engineered situation.	Act out the skill in a role-playing or engineered situation.

Set up scenarios and role-playing situations that allow the child to practice the skill in contrived situations. We've divided them into simple and more complex role-plays. It might be helpful to train peers for some of the role-plays.

Journal	
Where I was and what I was doing • at school in the gym • having a race	What I said or did when I won or lost • "Maybe next time!" • gave the winner a high five • got ready to race again

Figure 50. Sample journal card for winning and losing.

The simple role-plays are:
- Two actors participate in a spelling bee—one wins, one loses.
- Two actors compete in an obstacle course—one wins, one loses.
- Two actors play a game of tic-tac-toe—one wins, one loses.

Reverse roles and repeat the role-plays described above. Remember to provide the prompt of the visual choice board of appropriate comments when necessary.

For a more complex role-play, give students the following prompt with the scenarios below it:

Pretend you are playing a soccer game: The game is tied. One person is the goalie. One person is trying to kick the winning goal.
Scenario One: The player who kicks the ball gets it in the net, past the goalie, and wins the game! Everyone responds with celebrations and exciting comments about winning.
Scenario Two: The player kicks the ball and the goalie blocks it from going in the goal. The game stays tied and goes into overtime. The players respond with appropriate comments to the player who kicked the ball and didn't get it in the goal.

Challenge for Step 3. Praise students for their participation and work on the role-plays. Then, give them the challenge of completing one of three quick activities such as answering math facts, playing the card game War, and calling a flipped coin. Tell students,

Pick one and play the game or activity you choose with a partner. Remember to use appropriate comments after winning or losing. Look at your choice board for these comments when you need to. I'm going to give each of you 10 pennies. Place a penny on the comment that you use. You may say something different from what is on the board like we've practiced. Try to use a variety of comments so that your pennies are placed all over the board. Once everyone has used all 10 pennies, we will have our celebration!

When each child has met the challenge, provide a celebration ceremony similar to the one in Step 3 of Skill #1.

STEP 4

Use—Earning the Fourth Puzzle Piece

Framework Step	The Teacher Will:	The Children Will:
Step 4 **USE**	Teach the children to use the skill in natural settings.	Use the skill with others in a school or home setting.

Use activity-based instruction to embed opportunities to make appropriate comments about winning and losing. Activities could include field day, board games, spelling games, card games, math facts games, or recess games. Use self-management strategies to set up a goal for each child to make a specific number of appropriate comments during the week. Create a chart for children to use to keep track of their own appropriate comments. Use priming by showing children the choice board and letting them talk about which ones they might want to use in the upcoming activities.

Challenge for Step 4. Give students a journal card like the one in Figure 50. Then, say,

All of you have been doing a great job filling in your charts and making good choices with what you say whether you win or lose! Now it's time for your challenge. I'm going to give each of you a large index card called a "journal." It's divided into two columns. The first column says, "Where I was and what I was doing" and the second column says, "What I said or did when I won or lost." I want you to take your journal with you over the next 3 days and write down any games or activities that you play.

When each child has met the challenge, provide a celebration ceremony similar to the one in Step 4 of Skill #1.

STEP 5

Explain—Earning the Fifth Puzzle Piece

Framework Step	The Teacher Will:	The Children Will:
Step 5 EXPLAIN	Teach the children the rationale for using the skill.	Say why the skill is effective in interacting with others.

Building on Social Thinking® strategies, begin a discussion related to the importance of using the skill. Explain that one consideration is thinking about what others think and feel:

Teacher: Why is it important to make appropriate comments after a competitive activity, whether you win or lose?
Child 1: I feel happy when I win, but the person who didn't win may not feel happy. It's important to be nice to that person, too.
Child 2: If you say something nice, whether you win or lose, people may want to play again.
Teacher: Perfect! It's important to be kind to others and treat them with respect whether you win or lose. That's called being a good sport.

Continue on with the discussion about being a good sport. Create a graphic organizer in which each child describes words and actions related to being a good sport. You may want them to paste in pictures of winners and losers as well. Some items you might use in the graphic organizer include:

- Saying kind things even if someone loses.
- Learning to lose without losing your "cool."
- Treating others with respect.
- Remembering that "you win some, you lose some."
- Offering encouragement, not criticism.
- Winning without bragging.
- Losing without complaining.
- Learning to control your own reactions when losing is disappointing.

Challenge for Step 5. Praise students for using words and pictures to describe the concept of being a "good sport." Then challenge each of the students to create a cue card that demonstrates this concept with words, especially verbs, and pictures. Tell students, "This card will be just for you to keep as a reminder of what you can say and do to be a good sport." When each child has met the challenge, provide a celebration ceremony similar to the one in Step 5 of Skill #1.

STEP 6

Adjust—Earning the Sixth Puzzle Piece

Framework Step	The Teacher Will:	The Children Will:
Step 6 ADJUST	Teach the children to use flexible thinking and problem solving.	List and demonstrate an alternative action whenever the social skill is not effective.

Teach the children some alternative actions to use when the skill is not working. Start by finding out what they already know. Ask a question like, "What do you do if a friend or classmate is not being a good sport, even when you are?" If necessary, prompt answers like:

- Give encouragement to my friend like:
  - » "I know you lost the last one, but let's play again."
  - » "Let's just have fun playing the game."

- Ask your partner to be a good sport. Some things you might say are:
  - » "Let's be good sports and say nice things to each other."
  - » "I want to play the game with you, but if you keep saying things like that I'm going to stop playing with you."

Use cognitive behavioral interventions by teaching the children the interactions among actions, thinking, feeling, and the physical conditions in the body. For example, help a child develop a modified Incredible 5-Point Scale (see Figure 51) to teach children to recognize these relationships.

Ask students, "What if you are feeling so frustrated and angry that you want to hurt someone or something?" If necessary, shape answers such as: "I could do something like . . ."

- Take three deep breaths and count to 10 slowly.
- Tell my friends or teachers I need to take a short break.
- Ask to talk to a "safe" person such as a counselor, teacher, or administrator.
- Write out my thoughts and describe my feelings in a journal.

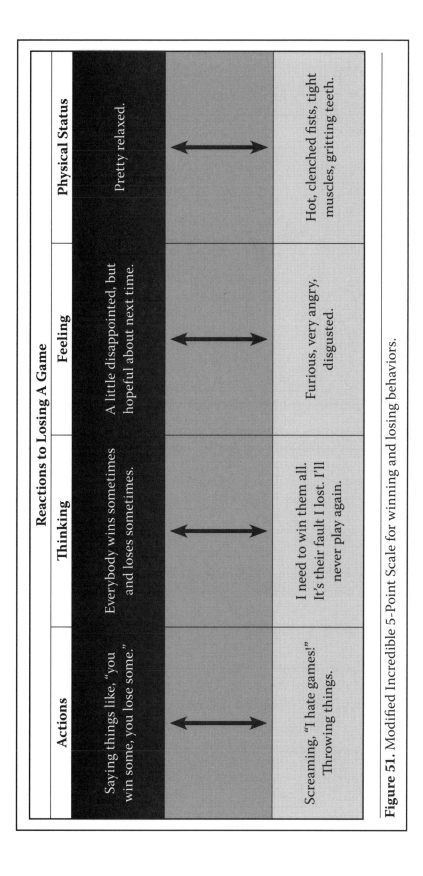

Reactions to Losing A Game			
Actions	**Thinking**	**Feeling**	**Physical Status**
Saying things like, "you win some, you lose some."	Everybody wins sometimes and loses sometimes.	A little disappointed, but hopeful about next time.	Pretty relaxed.
Screaming, "I hate games!" Throwing things.	I need to win them all. It's their fault I lost. I'll never play again.	Furious, very angry, disgusted.	Hot, clenched fists, tight muscles, gritting teeth.

Figure 51. Modified Incredible 5-Point Scale for winning and losing behaviors.

Figure 52. Relaxation techniques.

Consider teaching a routine using relaxation-training techniques. The routine should be individualized to meet the needs of the child, such as the one in Figure 52.

Challenge for Step 6. Remind students:

We have been discussing and practicing what we can say or do if:
○ we are being a good sport and someone else is not.
○ we feel angry when we lose.
○ someone isn't playing the way we think he or she should.

For your challenge, I want you to list and describe appropriate responses for each of the above situations. Then, you'll pick two to demonstrate for our group. When your lists and demonstrations are done, you'll have met your challenge!

When each child has met the challenge, provide a celebration ceremony similar to the one in Step 6 of Skill #1.

Skill #7: Helping Others

STEP 1
Play—Earning the First Puzzle Piece With Freeze Tag

Framework Step	The Teacher Will:	The Children Will:
Step 1 PLAY	Teach the children to play the game that requires the use of the targeted social skill.	Use the targeted social skill in a fun and engaging game.

Use the game Freeze Tag to teach the skill of helping others. To set up the game, assign children into two teams.

Directions for play. To play the game:

1. Mark out an area of play with boundaries.
2. One team is chosen to chase the other team.
3. When a player touches someone from the other team, he calls out "Freeze." The player must stand still and not move.
4. The player remains frozen until a player from his team comes and touches him and says "Sunshine." The player is free to run again.
5. After 5 minutes, swap out the teams, so the opposite team is in charge of freezing players.
6. *Alternative*: This game can also be played with one person chasing all of the other players. The remaining rules are the same.

Teaching the game. For quick learners or experienced players, explain:

You are the players and you have been divided into teams. One team will be chasers and the other team will be runners. When you are chasers, your goal is to touch as many members of the running team as possible. When you are runners, your goal is to stay away from the chasers and not get touched. Anyone who is touched has to freeze in place. When you are frozen, you can't move. You should freeze in a way that lets your team members know you can't move. (Demonstrate a frozen position such as a runner's stance.) Your team members can unfreeze you. They can run up to you, touch you, and say "Sunshine!" Sunshine melts the freeze and you can run again.

For early learners or new players, explain, "We're going to play Freeze Tag. Let's first practice freezing." Demonstrate by touching a colleague on the arm and saying, "See how she is frozen in place? She can't run anymore because she has to pretend that she is frozen right here." Use Discrete Trial Teaching and explain: "So, let's practice. Let's all march in place for a minute. When I say, 'freeze!' stop marching and stand very still." Practice this until all players understand how to freeze.

Then, explain:

We have two teams. Everybody on the blue team will try to touch people on the red team. You are the chasers. When you touch someone on the red team, that person will freeze. If you are on the red team, you will be the runners. You'll be trying to stay away from the chasers. So, let's practice. Start marching in place. Now, when someone on the blue team (a chaser) touches you, stop marching and freeze in your place.

Practice a few rounds individually and then practice as a group until everyone can demonstrate freezing in place when touched.

Next explain: "When you are frozen, you can't move. But, another person from your team can help you. That person can touch you on the arm and say, 'Sunshine!' When the person says, 'Sunshine!' you can move again." Practice a few rounds where team members unfreeze other team members. Before letting the children run, practice a few rounds where chasers touch the runners and other runners unfreeze their teammates. In some cases, do this individually with everyone watching. In other cases, you may be able to have two or three children practice at a time. Make sure all children understand the game before letting them start chasing and running. If they do not understand the game, it will deteriorate into a running free-for-all. It may also be helpful to use a visual schedule to help early learners understand the sequence of the game.

When starting the game, say,

We're starting with the blue team as chasers. Your job will be to chase the red team members who are the runners. Try to touch a runner and if you do, say, "Freeze!" When you are frozen, stay in place until a team member (another runner) comes to touch you and says "Sunshine!" Remember to try to help your friends by unfreezing them!

Challenge for Step 1. Tell students,

We have had so much fun playing the game Freeze Tag. I am going to see if you can remember how to be a runner and how to be a chaser. Everyone will get a turn to be both. When you can show me the rules of how to be a runner and how to be a chaser one time by yourself, you will have earned your first puzzle piece. And, the main thing I am watching for is to see if you can be helpers to your friends. Don't let anybody stay frozen! Let's play!

When each child can play the game independently, provide a celebration ceremony similar to the one in Step 1 of Skill #1.

STEP 2
Talk—Earning the Second Puzzle Piece

Framework Step	The Teacher Will:	The Children Will:
Step 2 TALK	Teach the children to name the social skill and say when it should be used.	Name the skill and, given a hypothetical situation, tell when it should be used.

Use direct instruction to teach children to name the new social skill of helping others. Ask students, "Remember when we played Freeze Tag? What happened in that game?" If necessary, shape answers such as:
- We were chasers and runners.
- We stayed frozen until someone came to help us.
- We touched people and froze them.
- Our friends could help us by saying, "Sunshine!"

Follow up with, "Our new social skill is called helping others. In the game, you helped others by unfreezing them. What are some other ways to help others?" Expect answers like:
- Pick up something your friend has dropped.
- Open the door for someone.
- Show them how to play a game.
- Fix something.

Ask students, "In the game, how did you know someone needed help?" If necessary, shape answers such as, "The person was frozen in place and not moving" or "The person called out, 'Help, please!'"
Then ask students, "At school, how might we know someone needs help?" Get students to think about answers like:
- When someone says "help."
- If you see someone struggling to do something.

Signs That My Friend Might Need Help!	
❑ Is my friend asking for help?	❑ Is my friend motioning for me to come over?
❑ Has my friend stopped working or covered his face with his hands?	❑ Has my friend fallen down and tears are coming down his face?

Figure 53. Checklist to tell when someone needs help.

- When my friends need something.

Finish up by asking students, "How do we know when it is a good time to help someone?" If necessary, shape answers such as:
- Ask them if they want help.
- Wait for a moment for them to ask for help.
- Look for signs like a gesture waving you over to the person.

Create a checklist like the one in Figure 53 to help students tell when to help someone. Continue by explaining to the children that, if they answer one or more of the questions with a yes, most likely their friend needs help. It would be appropriate to help their friend at those times.

Challenge for Step 2. Remind students of the game Freeze Tag and the new skill of helping others. Then, give them the challenge: "This week, I will be asking you some questions. I'll be looking for answers that name the skill and tell when to use it. I'll keep track and when you have 10 correct answers, you'll have met your challenge!" Your exchanges with students might sound like this:

Teacher: It was almost time to go to lunch. Phil was holding his lunch and his bag broke. His food rolled all over the floor. Julie picked up the food. What was Julie doing?
Child: Helping Phil.
Teacher: What's the name of our skill?
Child: Helping others.
Teacher: Fantastic! What makes you think Phil needed help?
Child: His food fell on the ground and it was almost time to go to lunch.
Teacher: Great thinking! Now, the teacher had her hands full of books. She wanted to go out the door. Should Jeremy help?
Child: Yes
Teacher: I agree! What could Jeremy do to help?
Child: Open the door.

Teacher: Wow! What a great answer! When is a good time to help others?
Child: When someone needs you to open a door.

When each child has met the challenge, provide a celebration similar to the one in Step 2 of Skill #1.

STEP 3
Act—Earning the Third Puzzle Piece

Framework Step	The Teacher Will:	The Children Will:
Step 3 ACT	Teach the children to demonstrate the skill in an engineered situation.	Act out the skill in a role-playing or engineered situation.

Use modeling to show children some scenarios for helping others. Demonstrate things like helping someone put on a coat, tying someone's shoe, and putting batteries in someone's toy. Then, set up role-playing situations by telling the children:

We're going to be Super Helpers! Your job is to wear the helper cape and help another person. All week long, we'll do role-plays and then we'll make movies. After we've made the movies, we'll watch and see how we did.

Possible scenarios include:
1. One person trying to open a container, other person asks, "Do you need help?" First person says, "Thanks!"
2. One person trying to put something on a high shelf, other person asks "Can I do that for you?" First person says, "Thanks!"
3. One person trying to write a note says, "How do you spell appreciate?" Second person finds the dictionary. First person says, "Thanks!"

Use Discrimination Training to teach children to recognize people who might need help. Set up such situations as:
1. One person is busy writing away; another person is looking puzzled. Which person might need help? How would you know? How could you help?
2. One person is washing dishes; another person is watching TV. Who might want help? How would you know? How could you help?

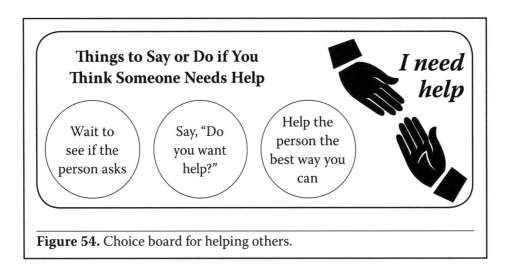

Figure 54. Choice board for helping others.

3. One person is standing near his locker pulling at the lock; another person is getting his books out of his locker. Who might want help? How would you know? How could you help?

Create a choice board like the one in Figure 54 to teach and then remind the children of the different ways to provide help. Create a group token economy by laminating a picture of helping hands. Then, cut the laminated picture into puzzle pieces and put a piece of Velcro™ on the back. Tell children, "When someone has provided help, I'll put a puzzle piece up on the board" (that has a corresponding picture with Velcro™ places for the puzzle pieces). Pair the placement of the puzzle piece with descriptive praise such as, "Wow! Kelsey was helping George get on his bike. We're putting up a puzzle piece in honor of Kelsey helping George!" When the hands are put together, provide a class celebration with a reward that all of the children enjoy.

Challenge for Step 3. Create a Kaper chart like the one in Figure 55 with jobs that need to be done in the classroom. Explain to students,

There is only one person assigned to do the task each day. But, each time, we really need two. If you volunteer to help, I will give you a high five and write your name as the Extra Helper on the chart. At the end of the week, I am going to take down the chart and see who has remembered to help others. When you have helped a friend two times with no reminder, you will have earned your next puzzle piece.

When each child meets the challenge, provide a celebration ceremony similar to the one in Step 3 of Skill #1.

Kaper Chart		
Task	**Assigned Helper**	**Extra Helper**
Empty Trash	James	
Hand Out Art Supplies	Alice	
Office Helpers	DJ	
Teacher Helpers	Walker	
Pet Helpers	Lee	

Figure 55. Kaper chart with classroom jobs.

STEP 4
Use—Earning the Fourth Puzzle Piece

Framework Step	The Teacher Will:	The Children Will:
Step 4 USE	Teach the children to use the skill in natural settings.	Use the skill with others in a school or home setting.

In the beginning, contrive a few situations in the natural environment using activity-based instruction. For example, set up play situations or projects that have a point where the children will need help. Perhaps you might provide a color-by-number page, but put the crayons in closed containers. Ask peers to pretend to have difficulty opening the container. In the beginning, prompt children to ask others if they need help.

Invite new peers to come play in the classroom. Direct them to get out things such as art supplies, but don't tell them where these things are located. Ask them to look around the room until the children notice that they need help locating supplies. Provide reminders to watch for opportunities for children to help others. Keep pictures of helpers posted and keep a chart that tracks instances of children helping other children. If possible, arrange for the children to help in a class of children who are younger or children who might need more help.

Challenge for Step 4. Give students a chart like the one in Figure 56. Tell students,

This week, I noticed that: **And, I helped!**

1. Ms. Anne needed help bringing books to the table.

2. Grant needed a paper towel to dry his hands.

3. Kristy dropped her pencil on the floor.

4. Grayson wanted more juice.

Figure 56. Helper chart.

Hello, Super Helpers! This week, I am going to look for friends who are helping others. I'll be watching you all week long and I'll be looking to see if you are helping others. When you have earned four helping hands on your chart, you will have earned this puzzle piece.

When each child has met the challenge, provide a celebration ceremony similar to the one in Step 4 of Skill #1.

STEP 5

Explain—Earning the Fifth Puzzle Piece

Framework Step	The Teacher Will:	The Children Will:
Step 5 **EXPLAIN**	Teach the children the rationale for using the skill.	Say why the skill is effective in interacting with others.

Use Social Thinking® principles to start a discussion, such as,

Friends, have you ever heard anyone say, "Treat others like you would like to be treated?" Or in other words, "Help your friends because sometimes you might need help?" Tell me, when you hear this, why is it important to help others? Some answers might start with:
- "My grandma said that's the Golden rule."
- "Do unto others as you would have them do unto you."

Yes, some would say this is what you are expected to do. This means that most people would do this if they saw someone needed help. Your mom might say, "It is the right thing to do or the right choice to make. So, if you feel like it is just the right thing to do, why do it?"

Expect answers like:
- It might help my friend feel better.
- If I help them, they might help me.
- If I help others, they will help me when I need help.

Respond with,

I think those all sound like great reasons to help others. It is not only what we are expected to do, but most of the time it feels good to do it. How do you think others feel when you help them?

Expect students to say things like, "They feel better" and "They are thankful." Then, ask students, "What do you think others think about you when you help them?" Expect answers like,
- They might think that I was nice.
- They might think that I was thoughtful.
- They might think that I cared about them.

Reinforce the learning by saying, "Yes, again, what you do impacts how others feel and think about you. Sometimes, remembering the Golden Rule makes a difference in how people see and feel about you."

Help students create a Social Story™ about why it is important to help others, like this one:

Helping Others
   When I am at school or home, I am usually around my friends, teachers, and family. I see people helping others. Sometimes people pick up things that other people have dropped. When they give them back, the person seems happy.
   Sometimes people carry things for other people. When they help, the other person usually says "thanks."
   Most of the time, it is important to try and help others because it is a nice thing to do. It is also good because it makes someone else happy or sometimes makes them feel better.
   Sometimes, when I am getting my things together to go home, and I don't know what the teacher said, I can ask my friend for help. It's good

to help others because there are times I may need help from a friend. If I give help, then when I need it, I might get help.

There are lots of reasons to help others. I will try and remember to help others when I can.

Challenge for Step 5. Tell students,

You have done a great job describing why it is important to help others. We made a terrific story. I want you to take this story and read it to a younger group of friends. After you have read the story to the children, I want you to help the children create a graphic organizer of why it is important to help others. When you have created your graphic organizer, bring it to me, and we will review it.

When each child has met the challenge, provide a celebration similar to the one in Step 5 of Skill #1.

STEP 6

Adjust—Earning the Sixth Puzzle Piece

Framework Step	The Teacher Will:	The Children Will:
Step 6 ADJUST	Teach the children to use flexible thinking and problem solving.	List and demonstrate an alternative action whenever the social skill is not effective.

Use Discrimination Training to teach whether or not a person is safe to ask for help or give help to. Begin a discussion such as this:

Teacher: Tell me, who are some safe people to ask for help?
Children: Mom, teacher.
Teacher: How do you know that they are safe?
Children: Because they are people I know.
Teacher: Now, I want you to listen to some stories and think about who might be safe in these situations. You are in a store and don't know where something is. You walk up to the cashier. Is that a person who is safe to ask for help?
Children: Yes.
Teacher: That's probably right! Why do you think he is safe to ask?

Children: Because he is at the cash register helping others and he has a badge on that lets me know he is working there.

Teacher: Fantastic! Think about this. You are at the store, and you don't know where something is. Next to you is someone whom you have never met. He doesn't have work clothes on or a badge. Is he safe to ask for help?

Children: Maybe not.

Teacher: Right. It is important to think about who is safe to ask for help. Now, I would like for you to create a chart (see Figure 57) that shows who your safe people are. Now that we know when we can ask for help and whom we can ask or give help to, let's talk about what to do if someone won't help you. Although it is an expected behavior to help others, sometimes you might come across a situation where someone will not help you. What do you think you should do?

Children: Find another friend to help me. Try to figure it out by myself. Find an adult who will help. Do something else.

Teacher: Those are all good ideas. Let's work together to record our ideas onto a cue card.

Talk to the children about what they can do if someone can't help them. Then, create a cue card like the one in Figure 58 for them to carry around or put in their desks.

Challenge for Step 6. Praise students for their work: "Friends, we have worked hard on figuring out whom to ask for help and what to do if someone won't help us." Then, set up the challenge for this step: "I'll be setting up some scenarios for you to demonstrate your flexible thinking skills. When you have demonstrated that you can use problem-solving skills in these role-playing situations, you will have met your challenge!" Possible scenarios include:

- You are outside on the playground with friends and your friend is hurt. There is a teacher and a stranger. Which person will you ask for help?
- You are playing with a toy. The battery is dead. You ask your dad to fix it, but he is busy cooking dinner. You ask your mom, but she is talking on the phone. What else can you do?
- You are working at school. You need help with your work, and the teacher is busy. You are not supposed to ask friends for help, and this is making you very angry! What else can you do?

When each child has met the challenge, provide a celebration ceremony similar to the one in Step 6 of Skill #1.

Who Can I Ask for Help?

At School	At Home	In the Community

Figure 57. Safe people chart.

If Someone Isn't Able to Help:	
I can try again to do it myself.	I can find another friend to ask
I can find another adult to ask.	I can then stop what I am doing and wait.
I can take some deep breaths to relax.	

Figure 58. Cue card for finding help.

Skill #8: Asking for Permission and Accepting "No" as an Answer

Play—Earning the First Puzzle Piece With Captain, May I?

Framework Step		The Teacher Will:	The Children Will:
Step 1 PLAY		Teach the children to play the game that requires the use of the targeted social skill.	Use the targeted social skill in a fun and engaging game.

Use the game Captain, May I? to teach the skill of asking for permission and accepting "no" as an answer. To set up the game:

1. Find an area (such as a hallway or large room) that is about 40 feet long and 10 feet wide.
2. Establish the "starting line" and the "finish line." Simple ways to do this are to use colored duct tape, plastic cones, or different colored carpet squares.

Teaching the game. Initially, the teacher should take the role of the Captain. Explain to the children that the goal of the game is to ask the Captain for permission, respond appropriately to the answer, and move toward the finish line. Start by teaching the children to ask the Captain one question and follow the directions that the Captain gives. Provide the children with a visual representation of possible questions they could ask the Captain.

Demonstrate how to ask a question and provide a model for following the instructions correctly. Some examples include:

- "Captain, may I take five baby steps forward?"
- "Captain, may I take two giant steps forward?"
- "Captain, may I take one twirling step forward?

Use Discrete Trial Training to teach children to take turns asking the Captain for permission. For example, the teacher should use the visual support to help children read the words "Captain, may I" at the top and then assist them in making a request. Require the children to use the complete question when asking for permission from the Captain (e.g., "Captain, may I hop forward 3 times?"). Following the models and demonstrations, allow the children to give other appropriate examples of asking the Captain a question. For example, "Captain, may I take three bunny hops forward?"

Provide modeling and prompting as necessary to help the children follow through with the specific actions they requested. If the Captain says, "Yes, you may," the child should hop forward like a bunny three times. It may also be necessary to teach the children to stay in place while the other children are taking their turns. Provide multiple opportunities for the children to practice making requests from the Captain.

Explain that the Captain will either say, "Yes, you may," or "No, you may not." If the Captain says, "No, you may not," then the Captain could add a different instruction for the child to follow. For example, if the child asks, "Captain, may I take three giant steps forward?" The Captain could say, "No, you may not. But you can take two baby steps forward." This is particularly useful when the Captain thinks a player is moving too close.

Provide multiple opportunities for the children to practice responding to both "yes" and "no" answers. Then, play the game with 3–5 children. It may help to have an adult or competent peer model play the game with the children. This person can get the game started by enthusiastically gaining the Captain's attention and saying, "My turn," or "I want to go first!"

Allow each child to take one turn. Once the turn-taking pattern has been established, continue taking turns until each player reaches the finish line. This will allow each player to experience success when learning the game. One way to establish a turn-taking pattern is for the Captain to write down a secret number between 1 and 10. Allow each player a chance to guess the correct number. The person who guesses closest to the number goes first. The player who guesses next to the closest goes second, and so on. If there is a tie, the captain could flip a coin and have one player call heads or tails. The player who calls the coin correctly goes first. Another suggestion for establishing a turn-taking pattern is to write down on index cards the words first, second, third, fourth, fifth, and so on. Fold the cards and place them in a bag. Allow the children to each draw one out and take turns according to the one they selected.

Give positive reinforcement throughout the game, using descriptive praise statements (paired with primary reinforcers when necessary). For example, say things like, "You did a super job asking the Captain for permission" or "I like the way you stayed calm when the Captain said, 'No you may not, but you can hop forward one time.'"

Challenge for Step 1. After several days of practice, tell the children they will now play the game on their own. Remind them of the rules: "Each one of you should use the phrase, 'Captain, May I' and add your request. Then you should follow the Captain's instruction of 'Yes, you may,' or 'No, you may not.'" Then, explain the challenge: "As you demonstrate these things, I will be putting stars by your name on the class poster board. When you have 10 stars by your name, you'll have met your challenge!" When each child has met the challenge, provide a celebration ceremony similar to the one in Step 1 of Skill #1.

STEP 2

Talk—Earning the Second Puzzle Piece

Framework Step	The Teacher Will:	The Children Will:
Step 2 **TALK**	Teach the children to name the social skill and say when it should be used.	Name the skill and, given a hypothetical situation, tell when it should be used.

After the children have played the game and earned the first puzzle piece, the teacher should lead a discussion similar to this:

Teacher: Remember playing Captain, May I? What did you do in that game?
Child 1: I hopped like a frog.
Child 2: I crossed the finish line.
Teacher: That's right! How did you get to hop and cross the finish line?
Child 2: I said, "Captain, may I?"
Child 1: When it was my turn I asked for what I wanted to do.
Teacher: Exactly right! We were using social skills to play the game. The first part of this social skill is called "asking for permission." There are a lot of times that we need to ask for permission, right?

Continue the discussion with the children by posing questions such as:

- What are some examples of questions you use to ask for permission? (To go places? To get items you want? To do something?)
- When are some times you need to ask for permission at school? At home?
- Are there better times to ask for permission to do something than other times?

Make a list on the board and give each child a sheet of paper with a picture of home on one side and school on the other. Help them draw or write out examples of situations for which they need to ask for permission.

Explain that the second part of the social skill is responding to "no." To address responding to "no," lead a discussion similar to this:

Teacher: How did the Captain answer you when you made a request?
Child 1: Most of the time the Captain said, "Yes, you may."
Child 2: Two times the Captain told me, "No, you may not" and told me to do something else.
Teacher: That's right! Sometimes you were told yes and other times you were told no. What did you do when you were told no?
Child 1: I just did what the Captain told me to do, but I didn't get to move as far.
Child 2: After he told me no, I tried to ask him again for what I wanted.

Use Direct Instruction techniques to teach and practice answers to questions such as these:

Teacher: When you ask for permission, what answers might you hear?
Children: Yes or no.
Teacher: What happens if the person says "yes"?
Children: We get to do it.
Teacher: What happens if the person says "no"?
Children: We have to wait or ask to do something else.

To summarize, tell children that the social skill is asking for permission *and* responding appropriately to no as an answer. Explain that it is important to ask, but it is necessary to understand that the answer might not always be yes. So, we have to listen to what people tell us. If the person says "yes," then we can do it. If the person says "no," then we have to wait or ask to do something else.

Challenge for Step 2. Tell students,

> We've been talking about the social skill that you used when you played the game Captain, May I? In order to earn your second puzzle piece, your challenge is to be able to name that social skill and tell me some times you would need to use it. All week long, I'll be asking questions about naming the social skill and when you would use it. I'll keep track on your token economy chart. When you have 10 good answers to my questions, you'll have met the challenge!

When each child has met the challenge, provide a celebration ceremony similar to the one in Step 2 of Skill #1.

STEP 3

Act—Earning the Third Puzzle Piece

Framework Step	The Teacher Will:	The Children Will:
Step 3 ACT	Teach the children to demonstrate the skill in an engineered situation.	Act out the skill in a role-playing or engineered situation.

Once the children can name the skill and talk about when to use it, set up role-play situations in which the children rehearse the skill in different scenarios.

Actor 1: *Child stands at chalkboard and pretends to be teaching the class.*
Actor 2: *Raises his hand, waits to be called on.* May I go to the restroom, please?
Actor 1: Sure. Thank you for raising your hand and asking first.

Actor 1: *Child sits at table and shows a book to the class (other actors) while acting as the teacher during reading instruction.*
Actor 2: *Raises hand.* Can I go to the computer now?
Actor 1: Not now. Remember, you have computer time after you answer your reading questions.
Actor 2: Okay. I will try to wait.

Actor 1: *Pretends to be Mom on the phone.*
Actor 2: *Walks in the room, sees Mom on the phone, and waits for her to get off.* As soon as Mom is off the phone, asks, Can I go swing outside?
Actor 1: Yes you can. I'll take you out there.

Actor 1: *Pretends to be Dad on the computer.*
Actor 2: *Walks in the room, sees Dad on the computer, and waits for him to get off.* As soon as Dad is off, asks, Can I go swing outside?
Actor 1: Not right now. We're leaving in a few minutes.
Actor 2: Well, okay. I guess I can find something else to do. *Sits down and looks at a magazine.*

In the beginning, ask the children to volunteer for the roles. Provide enough practice sessions so that all children get to play all parts. When necessary, assign roles to ensure that everyone does everything.

After the children are comfortable with these, involve them in writing scripts for additional role-plays. It's fun to have a bag of props and allow children to think of ways to use them. Train peers to be models or to participate in the role-plays.

Challenge for Step 3. Praise students for their work on the skill: "You all have done a great job participating in the role-plays and demonstrating that you know how to respond appropriately to 'yes' and 'no' in the situations we practiced. Way to go!" Then, explain the challenge: a show and tell session. Provide these details:

I have several neat items available for you to pick from. Each of you will choose an item to *show* your classmates and *tell* them why you picked it. Your classmates are going to ask you for permission to hold, look at, or play with the items that you chose. Sometimes you might answer "yes" and occasionally the answer could be "no." I'll be watching for acceptable responses to both answers just like you practiced in the role-plays. After everyone has had a turn in show and tell and has demonstrated acceptable responses to "yes" or "no," we will have a celebration.

STEP 4

Use—Earning the Fourth Puzzle Piece

Framework Step	The Teacher Will:	The Children Will:
Step 4 USE	Teach the children to use the skill in natural settings.	Use the skill with others in a school or home setting.

Use generalization strategies to help the children use the skills in the natural setting. For example, set up opportunities to ask for permission in different settings, with different people, and at different times. When necessary, prompt and reinforce the child to use the skill in these additional settings. Then, fade the prompts out systematically, but continue reinforcing correct use of the skill in natural settings.

Create a cue card like the one in Figure 59 to help children ask for permission in their environment. This can be placed in several settings and serve as a way to transfer stimulus control. Teach children to use self-management strategies with the cue card. Initially, tell the children to confirm with the adult that the steps were followed correctly. They can then put their plus sign in the appropriate box. Arrange for the children to exchange the card for more tangible reinforcers for every five boxes that are filled. Be sure to provide plenty of social praise before providing the tokens and primary reinforcers.

Also, prime children by reminding them of the expectations and the steps for using the skill prior to entering the natural setting. This can take place in the form of a brief reminder. For instance, the teacher in the general education classroom could say, "When you need to go to the restroom or get water during work time, raise your hand and ask me," or "When you finish your work, ask for permission before going to the computer."

Challenge for Step 4. Remind students of how they have used the skill: "You have been practicing asking for permission from different people and in different places throughout the school. You have done a super job of giving appropriate responses whether the answer is 'no' or 'yes!'" Then, give them the challenge for this step: a blank version of the cue card in Figure 58, with five empty boxes. Tell them, "I want you to practice this same skill at home. Use it with your family, neighbors and friends." Children should put a plus sign in the box each time they ask for permission to go somewhere, do something, share something, order something, or so forth. Remind students to "be sure to accept the answer you are given." When each child has met the challenge and marked off five boxes on the cards, provide a celebration ceremony similar to the one in Step 4 of Skill #1.

Asking for Permission in the Classroom	
1. Look around and see if it's a good time to ask for permission.	
2. Raise my hand and wait calmly to be called on.	
3. Ask politely when I'm called on.	
4. Respond in an acceptable way to the answer.	

Place a + in the box each time I successfully follow the steps for asking for permission.

☐　　☐　　☐　　☐　　☐

Figure 59. Cue card for asking for permission.

STEP 5

Explain—Earning the Fifth Puzzle Piece

Framework Step	The Teacher Will:	The Children Will:
Step 5 **EXPLAIN** 	Teach the children the rationale for using the skill.	Say why the skill is effective in interacting with others.

Use strategies and language from Social Thinking® to help children create T-charts of expected behaviors versus unexpected behaviors for asking for permission and responding to "no" (see Figure 60). Explain that expected behaviors are behaviors that people usually do and that other people think we will probably do. Unexpected behaviors are behaviors that don't usually belong in this place or at this time. When we behave as other people expect us to, they might have good thoughts about us. In fact, they might not even notice us. But, when we

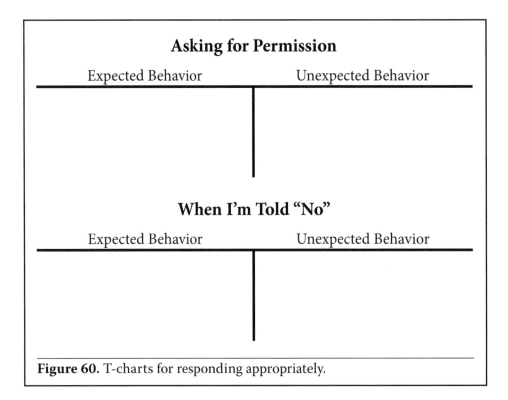

Figure 60. T-charts for responding appropriately.

do something unexpected, people pay attention to us. They might have negative thoughts about us and think that we are acting in a strange way.

Summarize the activity with a discussion such as this: "These are great charts of expected and unexpected behavior! So, let's look at responding to 'no.' Why is it important to respond using expected behavior?" Expect answers like:

- If I stay calm, I may get what I want later.
- When I'm polite instead of demanding, I am more likely to get the things I want.
- People might have good thoughts about me.
- If I don't, people might have negative thoughts about me.

Challenge for Step 5. Praise students for their hard work. Then, remind them of the skill they are learning: "We have been discussing ways to respond when you are told 'no,' 'not now,' or 'wait.' We've made lists of expected versus unexpected responses as a group." Then, pose the challenge to the students: "I want each of you to create your own lists describing what you can do when you are told 'no,' 'not now,' or 'wait.'" You may want to facilitate this list-making in groups or with graphic organizers. When each child has met the challenge, provide a celebration ceremony similar to the one in Step 5 of Skill #1.

STEP 6

Adjust—Earning the Sixth Puzzle Piece

Framework Step	The Teacher Will:	The Children Will:
Step 6 ADJUST	Teach the children to use flexible thinking and problem solving.	List and demonstrate an alternative action whenever the social skill is not effective.

Provide scenarios to the students in which they practice discriminating whether or not it is a good time to ask for permission. Begin with the scenarios below.

- You want to go outside and ride your bike and you need an adult to go with you when you ride. Your mom is home; however, she is taking a shower. What would you do?
- The teacher is standing in front of the class teaching. You really want to ask permission to tell the class about your birthday party. What do you do?

Some possible answers include:

- I would wait to ask her when she gets out of the shower and is dressed. I would practice playing the piano while I waited. I could read a book instead.
- I can wait until she's finished talking to the class and raise my hand. I can ask her during recess.

Reinforce the child for flexible thinking and being able to discriminate between a "good time to ask" versus a "time to wait or do something different." Use Social Thinking® strategies and a consequence map to teach the children expected versus unexpected behaviors when asking for permission and accepting "no." In the consequence map include consequences for behavior, thinking, and feeling (see Figure 61).

Challenge for Step 6. Tell students,

Remember our consequence map? It provided examples of consequences for expected behavior and consequences for unexpected behavior in response to being told "no." In this challenge, each of you will create your own consequence map! You can use words and pictures that describe the expected and unexpected behaviors and the consequences. Be sure to include how you will be thinking and feeling.

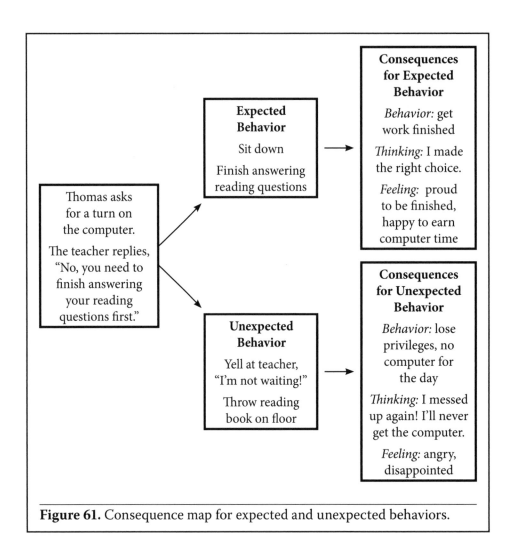

Figure 61. Consequence map for expected and unexpected behaviors.

Make the challenge fun by helping the students create their own maps using collages or drawings to represent behaviors and consequences. When each child has met the challenge, provide a celebration ceremony similar to the one in Step 6 of Skill #1.

Skill #9: Talking With Others

Play—Earning the First Puzzle Piece
With Get to Know You Bingo

Framework Step	The Teacher Will:	The Children Will:
Step 1 PLAY	Teach the children to play the game that requires the use of the targeted social skill.	Use the targeted social skill in a fun and engaging game.

Use the game Get to Know You Bingo to teach children the skill of "talking with others." The purpose of this activity is to provide opportunities for the children to approach other people, ask questions, wait for responses, learn interesting information and facts about others, answer questions, and ultimately have conversations.

To set up the game, create a simple Bingo card with several interesting facts. Depending on the number of children playing the game, the cards could be 3 x 3, 4 x 4, or 5 x 5. Use prior knowledge of the children to generate a portion of the facts (if available) and list additional general facts such as the ones in the sample Get to Know You Bingo card found in Figure 62. Be sure to set up the list so that it includes interests, characteristics, and experiences of the children who will be playing the game. Begin with the obvious likes and dislikes, positive characteristics, and interesting experiences.

Teaching the game. For early learners or new players, demonstrate the game with the following steps:

1. Use one card and play the game as a group. Begin with children seated in a semicircle.
2. Read a characteristic, "Likes animals," and then ask several individuals if they like animals. To model the potential need to ask several people before finding one whose name can be written on the card, it might be good to start by asking several children who will probably say "no." When a child says "yes," ask the child to write his or her name on the corresponding square on the card.
3. Ask a child to read a second item, "Likes to roller skate." That child is prompted to ask individuals, "Do you like to roller skate?" Once that child has found someone who likes to roller skate and has gotten that person to write his or her name on the card, the next child is prompted

Has been to a waterpark	Likes the color orange	Has a pet goldfish	Rode a roller coaster	Has a large family
Wants to be a firefighter	Has dressed up like Batman	Can do a cartwheel	Likes to roller skate	Wants to be a teacher
Likes to sing in the car	Has a dog and a cat	**FREE**	Can make origami figures	Has on older brother and sister
Has made friendship bracelets	Can play hopscotch	Has a collection of trains	Can dive off a diving board	Likes the color purple
Can count to 10 in Spanish	Likes superheroes	Can ride a bike	Eats cheese pizza	Can do a hoola hoop

Figure 62. Sample Get to Know You Bingo card.

to begin asking a question about the third item. Each child should practice asking questions from the card and waiting for responses.

4. After every child has had an opportunity to practice, a new Get to Know You Bingo card should be given to each child to play the game.

For more advanced players:

1. Explain to the children that they will learn to play a Bingo game that will help them learn more about each other by asking questions.

2. Pass out a sample Get to Know You Bingo card to each child, along with a pencil. Consider using a different sample card than the one the children will be using to play the game. Model the use of a Bingo card with, for example, color words. Provide an example of approaching and asking with the sample card. For example, approach Abigail and ask, "Abigail, do you like the color purple?" If Abigail says, "Yes, I do like the color purple," then ask Abigail to write her first name in that box on the card.

3. Allow the children to practice with the sample card by approaching other children and asking a questions such as "Is your favorite color

red?" Once they find someone who meets the description, they should practice asking the friend to sign his or her name in the appropriate box.

4. Explain that the goal is to get a full row of signatures—horizontally, vertically, or diagonally. Once that happens, the person shouts "Bingo!" and wins the game. Provide a model of a card with a full row of signatures.

5. Tell the children that once they fill up a row with signatures, they will introduce the person whose name is in each box and tell an interesting fact about that person. Model this by introducing Abigail, saying, "This is Abigail, and she likes the color purple."

6. After the children have practiced with the sample card, give each child a card that has interesting facts on it. Direct the children to begin playing the game. Offer an instruction such as the one below:

You are going to approach other people and ask them questions. Your goal is to find people who meet the descriptions on the list. When we start, you should read a description, "Likes animals," and start asking your friends this question: "Do you like animals?" If the person says "no," say, "Thanks anyway!" If the person says "yes," say, "Great! Please sign your first name in the box." Remember, the goal is to get a complete row of signatures and shout, "Bingo!" After everyone fills up a row, we'll take turns introducing each other and telling interesting facts that we learned about each other.

Variations.
- Work in teams of two or three to complete the list.
- Go to other classrooms or other parts of the school to find people who meet the descriptions on the list.

Challenge for Step 1. Give students praise for their play, then provide them with the challenge. Each student will get a new Bingo card and will play the game without any help from the teacher. Challenge students to get signatures from at least two different people than the ones who signed their card last time. Tell students, "After the game is finished and you introduce the people who signed your card, you'll have met your goal!" When each child has met the challenge, provide a celebration ceremony similar to the one in Step 1 of Skill #1.

STEP 2
Talk—Earning the Second Puzzle Piece

Framework Step	The Teacher Will:	The Children Will:
Step 2 **TALK**	Teach the children to name the social skill and say when it should be used.	Name the skill and, given a hypothetical situation, tell when it should be used.

After the children have played the game Get to Know You Bingo and earned puzzle piece #1, the teacher should lead a discussion with the group about what they did in the game such as the following:

Teacher: Remember when we played the game Get to Know You Bingo? What happened in the game?
Child 1: We got a Bingo card of interesting facts and descriptions on it.
Child 2: We walked up to other people and asked them questions.
Child 3: We wrote our first name in the squares by things we liked or did.
Teacher: Exactly! And how did you find out who could write in the square?
Child 1: We asked each person questions.
Child 2: We asked other people what they liked.
Teacher: Excellent! And what happened when you found someone who met the description?
Child 1: I asked my friend to write her name in the square by something she liked.
Child 3: I introduced the person to the group and told something he liked.
Teacher: Yes! You learned interesting facts about each other by approaching each other and asking questions. Then you introduced each other based on the interesting facts that you learned. The skill we practiced is called "talking with others." Often we begin talking with others by asking them questions. They answer. We tell them something. They respond. That's what talking with others is.

Use Direct Instruction techniques to teach the children to name the skill and say when they would use it. If appropriate, include trained peers in teaching sessions to model appropriate answers. Ask for short responses, maintain a rapid pace, and provide a high rate of success with such questions as:

- What's the name of our skill? (talking with others)

- When might you want to talk with others? (In the cafeteria)
- When's another time you might want to talk with others? (At recess)
- When else? (When you want to know something about the person)
- Like what? (Age, birthday, or favorite color)

Ask these questions by alternating among individuals and use lots of positive reinforcement. To keep children actively involved, periodically throw in questions that require a choral response. Make these sessions positive and fun.

Challenge for Step 2. Thank the students for doing so well, then share the first part of the challenge with them: "I'll be asking you questions all week long and I'll be keeping a record of your answers. When I have five answers from each person, we'll review them in our group." Then, share the second part of the challenge: "Then, on a piece of paper, I'll ask you to list three times when it's important to talk with others. When you have five good answers and three times on your paper, you'll have met your challenge!" When each child has met the challenge, provide a celebration ceremony similar to the one in Step 2 of Skill #1.

STEP 3

Act—Earning the Third Puzzle Piece

Framework Step	The Teacher Will:	The Children Will:
Step 3 ACT	Teach the children to demonstrate the skill in an engineered situation.	Act out the skill in a role-playing or engineered situation.

Once the children can name the skill of "talking with others" and can describe when to use it, set up role-play situations in which the children rehearse the skill in different scenarios. Practice and rehearse each scenario until both actors can perform it independently.

Actor 1: *Child bouncing a ball outside at recess.*
Actor 2: *Walks up to child.* Do you like to play sports?
Actor 1: I do. I play on a basketball team. Do you play sports?
Actor 2: Yes. I like soccer and play on a soccer team.

Actor 1: *Coloring a picture at a table.*
Actor 2: *Sits down to color a picture also. Looks at Actor 1.* What's your favorite color?

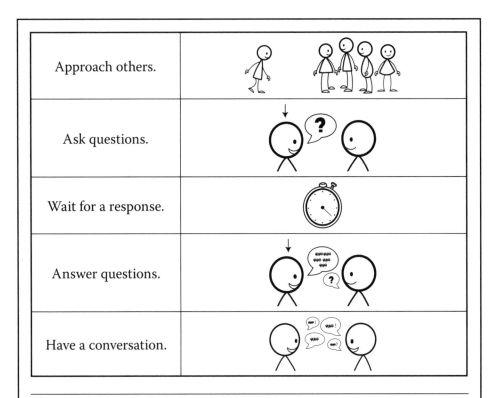

Figure 63. Visual schedule for talking with others.

Actor 1: I like blue. What's your favorite color?
Actor 2: My favorite color is orange.

Actor 1: *Sitting at the table pretending to eat lunch.*
Actor 2: *Sits down and pretends to eat lunch. Looks at Actor 1.* What's your favorite movie?
Actor 1: I just saw the new Spider-Man movie. What movies do you like?
Actor 2: I like Spider-Man and Batman movies.

To teach children to participate in role-playing activities, it may be helpful to consider one or more of the following strategies to help them to understand what to do. First, typical peers can model the role-plays. Make sure that children have the opportunity to play all the different roles. Another strategy to consider is to make a video of the children interacting in the role-play. Provide them with feedback regarding the following behaviors: approaching and orienting toward the communicative partner, asking questions using an appropriate tone of voice, waiting for a response, and responding to questions that are asked. Finally, you can use a visual schedule (see Figure 63) to help the children recall the sequence of events.

Challenge for Step 3. Praise students for their work: "You all have done a super job being actors and actresses and rehearsing having short conversations with each other." Then, copy the visual schedule in Figure 63 and cut the copies into pieces so that the steps are mixed up. Tell students, "Your challenge will be to paste the pictures onto your paper in the proper order. That way, I'll know that you are remembering the steps for talking with others." After the students have done this, make movies of them showing the schedule, explaining the steps, and then demonstrating one role-play for the skill. When each child has met the challenge, provide a celebration ceremony similar to the one in Step 3 of Skill #1.

STEP 4
Use—Earning the Fourth Puzzle Piece

Framework Step	The Teacher Will:	The Children Will:
Step 4 USE	Teach the children to use the skill in natural settings.	Use the skill with others in a school or home setting.

To help children talk with others in the natural environment, use social scripts as prompts for conversations. Use these scripts the way an actor uses them to learn lines for a play. Some children may need the scripts for a long time, while others may only need them briefly. When possible, fade these written prompts systematically as children become proficient at talking with others without the scripts. If necessary, provide trained peer models to be partners while practicing the scripts. In the beginning, the entire conversation may need to be scripted. Later, the children may only need prompts for getting conversations started. Sample conversation starters include:
- I like to watch movies.
- Playing outside is fun.
- I collect toy dinosaurs.
- My favorite TV show is . . .

Once children are proficient in starting conversations and maintaining a discussion with two or three exchanges, use self-management strategies to help children maintain longer conversations without using scripts. Teach children to approach a peer, say one or two things about a topic, then ask a question. For some children, you may need to provide steps on a cue card. For others, you may need to use priming to review the steps shortly before possible conversations.

The Challenge for Step 4. Give students a blank chart with the four steps on the cue card and check boxes for three situations. Tell students,

> You have been practicing having conversations with your friends by choosing a "conversation starter" that is interesting and fun to talk about! I like the way that you are practicing the four steps from your cue card. Now it's time for your challenge to earn puzzle piece #4. You will each have a chart that gives you a reminder of the four steps we just practiced. I want you to pick three different places at school, besides our classroom, where you will follow the four steps. Write in the conversation starter you choose for that location on your chart before you begin the conversation. For example, you could decide to bring up a topic about movies in the cafeteria with the student you sit across from. After you use the four steps, I want you to rate how you did and how successful you think the conversation was. When the charts are filled in for three different places, you will have met your challenge!

When each child has met the challenge, provide a celebration ceremony similar to the one in Step 4 of Skill #1.

STEP 5

Explain—Earning the Fifth Puzzle Piece

Framework Step	The Teacher Will:	The Children Will:
Step 5 EXPLAIN	Teach the children the rationale for using the skill.	Say why the skill is effective in interacting with others.

Ask children, "Why do you think it's important talk with others?" If necessary, shape answers such as:

- So we can learn something about them.
- We can find out if we have any common interests.
- If we ask people questions and know some things about them, then we have something to talk about.
- Other people like for us to be interested in them and they might like to talk to us more if we ask them questions.

Use a Social Story™ like the one below to help children understand the importance of talking with others.

Talking With Others Helps in Making Friends

Most people think that talking with others is a good way to make friends. Friends usually talk about what they like to do, where they like to go, and what they like to eat. Sometimes they talk about what they don't like. They might talk about a movie they didn't like watching or a book they didn't like reading.

When people talk to each other they learn more about what each one likes. Friends sometimes like the same things. They might like watching the same movies or playing the same games.

Talking with others also helps us learn what people don't like, too. That can be important in making friends, too. Friends don't always have to like the same things or do the same things, but it is helpful to know. That way, the friends don't push their friends do things they don't like.

I will try to talk with others. I hope this will help me make friends.

Help children create their own Social Stories™ related to the importance of talking with others. Read the stories with the children each day, especially prior to activities in which they will be talking and interacting with others.

Use Comic Strip Conversations™ to help children see the importance of talking with others. While explaining the following to the children, draw speech bubbles and thinking balloons and figures that represent:

- Two people having a conversation with three exchanges on a topic of interest to both
- One person talking and the other person staying silent
- One person talking and the other person walking away
- Two people talking about something and then going to do something fun

Challenge for Step 5. Remind students of the skill by saying, "We've been talking about why it's important to talk with others." Then, present the challenge:

We're going to make collages of people talking to each other. You can look through these magazines and cut out pictures of people. Then, you can use speech bubbles and thinking balloons to represent talking with others. Each person needs to show at least three conversations. When you have finished, you'll make a list of five things that you can find out by talking with others. We'll post our finished collages and lists on the walls and then you'll have met your challenge!

When each child has met the challenge, provide a celebration ceremony similar to the one in Step 5 of Skill #1.

STEP 6

Adjust—Earning the Sixth Puzzle Piece

Framework Step	The Teacher Will:	The Children Will:
Step 6 ADJUST	Teach the children to use flexible thinking and problem solving.	List and demonstrate an alternative action whenever the social skill is not effective.

Using cognitive intervention strategies, start a discussion by asking the following:

- What could you do if . . .
  - » someone doesn't want to answer you or talk?
  - » someone talks too long and you are tired of listening?

- What are some ways to recognize facial expressions that might be indicating boredom, excitement, and interest?
- How does body language help us determine whether to continue talking with others?

Watch short video examples of movie clips, TV shows, or videos the children have previously made. Turn the volume all the way down. Help the children write down all of the different emotions they observe on the faces of one particular actor. Discuss their gestures and expressions and how they indicate their various feelings and emotions.

Help the children complete these sentences:
- I may be talking too long or too much about myself when . . .
- I should continue on in the conversation when . . .
- I can make guesses about what others are thinking by . . .
- Some good things to do to understand others are . . .

Work with the class to make a large consequence map. Help the children list, describe, and draw pictures of the following: (a) what potentially happens when we take turns in a conversation by following the steps we've described and both (all) people are interested in the topic, and (b) what potentially happens if we talk to others about topics that only we are interested in and we talk for a long time. Post the map in the classroom.

Then, use the following four steps of Social Thinking® to help children in understanding others (Winner, 2008):
- Step 1: Think about the people who are near you

- Step 2: Think about why the person is near you
- Step 3: Think about what other people may be thinking about you
- Step 4: Change and modify your own behavior

Present the two scenarios below to the children, one at a time. Ask them to highlight, circle, or label how Abigail and Kevin demonstrate each of the four steps.

During center time, Abigail was building a castle with blocks. She saw Michael standing nearby, watching her build. She looked at Michael and thought about how close he was. She then remembered that yesterday the two of them shared the blocks and built the castle together. Abigail thought that Michael might want to build with her again today. She looked at Michael and said, "Do you want to build with me today?" Michael said, "Yes," and the two of them built castles and bridges throughout the rest of center time.

Kevin was walking in line with his class to the computer lab. He noticed two girls standing near the water fountain giggling. At first Kevin wanted to yell at them and tell them to quit laughing at him. Then he thought about why he was in the hallway and why they were in the hallway. He was heading to the computer lab and they had just come out of the bathroom. Kevin realized the girls weren't even looking at him. Then he remembered that he was sent to the office yesterday for yelling at two other kids in the hallway because he thought they were laughing at him when they weren't. Kevin thought about what the girls would think if all of a sudden he just yelled at them. They might look at him in a surprised sort of way, yell back, and think he was rude. He decided to just keep walking and not say anything. Kevin headed on to computer lab, which was his favorite special class, and successfully completed his project.

Challenge for Step 6. Remind students of what they've learned: "We have been looking at scenarios and discussing steps to take that will help us understand what other people may be thinking. This will help us to be flexible and adjust our behavior while having conversations." Provide them with further practice in the challenge by asking them to either create a short skit or draw a simple cartoon that demonstrates a situation in which they are having a conversation with another person and they changed their behavior and became flexible in response to the behavior of that person. When students are finished, have them share their products with the group, thus earning the next puzzle piece. When each child has met the challenge, provide a celebration ceremony similar to the one in Step 6 of Skill #1.

Skill #10: Pretending With Others

Play—Earning the First Puzzle Piece With Paper Bag Skits

Framework Step	The Teacher Will:	The Children Will:
Step 1 **PLAY**	Teach the children to play the game that requires the use of the targeted social skill.	Use the targeted social skill in a fun and engaging game.

Use the game Paper Bag Skits to teach children to engage in pretend play with others. Although there are other social skills such as turn taking and joint attention being practiced in this game, the main focus of the game is to create opportunities to take on a role and pretend. Gather the following materials prior to starting the game:

- large paper bags,
- props that can fit in a bag,
- a timer (for some versions), and
- a visual schedule for the steps involved in playing the game (see Figure 64).

Directions for play. To play the game:
- Separate the children into groups of three or four.
- Arrange the room so that the groups will have space to move and perform.
- Give each team a bag with props.

Variations.
- The bag of props could be filled with items that are closely related (e.g., Barbie™, Barbie™ bed, and Barbie™ chair).
- The bag of props could be filled with items that are not related at all (e.g., Barbie™, orange, pencil, and stuffed animal).
- The skit also could be scripted, drafted at the time, or drafted after being given a topic to use.

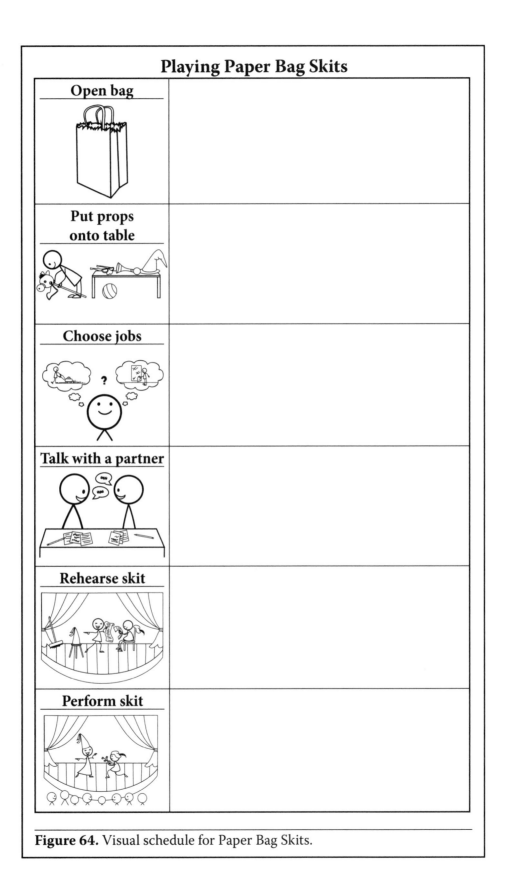

Figure 64. Visual schedule for Paper Bag Skits.

Teaching the game. For quick learners or experienced players, explain:

In this great game, your group is going to make up a skit. A skit is a little play that you create yourselves. It's like the role-plays we've been doing, but in this case, you have some props you can use for pretending! You'll get to look in the bag, take out the items, and then use the items in a skit. It's your job to think of the skit and practice it with your team members. When you are finished, you will act out the story in front of the other teams.

For inexperienced players, explain: "In this game, you'll take out the objects and practice the skit by taking turns reading the script. A skit is a little play and the scripts are the lines of the actors. Watch me!" While the children are watching, take the first prop and the first script card out of the bag. For example, take out a stuffed dog. Hand the bag to your colleague or a trained peer. Ask that person to take out the second prop, a dog bowl, and the second script. Take turns reading the script, such as: "My dog's name is Knox and he is very thirsty." (Shake Knox and make panting sounds.) Wait for your partner to respond, reading: "Look, here's a water bowl. Let's let Knox drink from the bowl." Then read: "Knox is sleepy now." (Put Knox down and make snoring sounds.) Assign partners and let each pair of children practice the same skit just demonstrated. Then, tell children they should take out the props from the bag, read the scripts, and act out the parts. Give them the schedule in Figure 64.

Play this game repetitively over a period of several weeks. In the beginning, practice the same skits again and again. Then, vary the props so that children are pretending with a variety of characters such as animals, dolls, and action figures. Expand the other props, too, so the characters will be in lots of pretend settings. These pretend settings might be out in space, on the playground, at the house, or in the mall. Use modeling when necessary, but as soon as possible, let the children create their own skits and perform them. As children become proficient in working with partners, increase the group to three or four. In addition, help them expand simple pretending into longer interactions among their pretend characters.

Challenge for Step 1. Tell students,

Hello actors! You've been doing great with your Paper Bag Skits! It's time for your challenge! You will meet your challenge by creating a brand new skit from props you haven't seen before. I'll make a movie and when you have finished your skit, we'll watch it on screen! When we've finished watching it, you'll have met your challenge!

When each child has met the challenge, provide a celebration ceremony similar to the one in Step 1 of Skill #1.

STEP 2
Talk—Earning the Second Puzzle Piece

Framework Step	The Teacher Will:	The Children Will:
Step 2 TALK	Teach the children to name the social skill and say when it should be used.	Name the skill and, given a hypothetical situation, tell when it should be used.

Ask children, "Remember when we played Paper Bag Skits? What did we do in the game?" Shape answers such as "We took things out of a bag and made up a skit" and "We thought of a story with the things from the bag."

Remind children of a few of their skits, saying something like:

I remember that Gina's group had a stuffed dog, plastic bone, and a small plastic dog bowl. What was your story? That's right! I remember you pretended your dog was thirsty and you let him drink some water from the bowl. Then, you pretended that your dog was sleepy.

Follow up on the experience by asking children a question such as, "So, in this game, what were you doing?" Shape answers such as:

- Making believe the dog was thirsty.
- Pretending the dog was sleepy.
- Acting like the dog was drinking the water.

Remind students of the social skill (pretending with others) being used. Tell them, "This is a fun skill because you can make up games to play with friends. You can act them out with different voices and actions and you can make believe that stuffed animals, dolls, and action figures are real."

Use Direct Instruction to provide practice in identifying the skill.

Teacher: When someone asks you to be a superhero and asks you to put on a red blanket, what are they asking you to do?
Children: Pretend to be a superhero.
Teacher: Right—they want you to use your imagination and be a super-hero. If you have a stuffed Cat in the Hat and a friend puts the hat on the cat and says, "I am the Cat in the Hat," what is he doing?
Children: Using the stuffed Cat in the Hat to pretend and make a story.
Teacher: Fantastic!

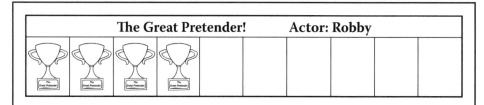

Figure 65. Token economy chart with rewards for pretending with others.

Continue with examples like this one until the children are responding quickly and correctly. This sequence provides a great lead into a series of interactions such as this:

Teacher: Okay, thinkers! When would you use this skill of pretending? Did the examples above give you any ideas?
Children: In a play.
Teacher: Outstanding! Anything else?
Children: Writing a story.
Teacher: Yes, sometimes it is great to pretend. I bet someone else has another idea.
Children: When playing games with friends.
Teacher: Right!

Challenge for Step 2: Praise students for their work, then give them the chart in Figure 65. Tell them to expect a social skills time every day and that you will watch them pretend with their friends before asking them to name the social skill and tell you when it could be used. Use the chart to set up a fun way to record their progress: "When you tell me about the social skill, I'll put an Oscar picture on your chart. An Oscar is an award that movie stars get! When you have 10 Oscars, you'll have met your challenge!" When each child has met the challenge, provide a celebration ceremony similar to the one in Step 2 of Skill #1.

STEP 3
Act—Earning the Third Puzzle Piece

Framework Step	The Teacher Will:	The Children Will:
Step 3 ACT	Teach the children to demonstrate the skill in an engineered situation.	Act out the skill in a role-playing or engineered situation.

Tell students about the next task: "Okay, great pretenders! Remember when we played Paper Bag Skits? That game helped us practice pretending with others. We are going to practice this by acting out stories in a play."

Use activity-based instruction to embed practicing this skill within a classroom routine. Choose books that are familiar and of interest to the children. Short stories or plays such as "Goldilocks and the Three Bears" are excellent. For older students, *James and the Giant Peach* or *Charlotte's Web* might be good choices. Use illustrations to create a visual schedule to help children remember what happens in the stories.

Allow all of the children to play each role in the stories for extra practice. Provide a review of the group's performance by using video modeling. Have the children find two times in the video where they were pretending with their peers using their best body movements and language for the role. Ask the students to describe what they were doing that made it their best. Record and review the characteristics on a list with the entire group. For instance, the characteristics might be listed like this:

- Our words showed that we were _____.
- Our bodies showed that we didn't know each other.
- Their actions showed that they were all surprised.

Challenge for Step 3: Tell students,

We've been working on pretending with others in the plays! Your challenge is to pick out your favorite book with your group and act out the story. You can use costumes and props. We will figure out what book your team is acting out and what role each actor is playing. The audience will be provided with a choice board for all of the roles for the game from which they can guess. When we guess your story, you'll have met your challenge!

To help facilitate this challenge, ask each of the groups which story they are representing and then create a choice board for the class of which stories they can guess as the skits are being presented. When each child has met the challenge of acting in his or her group, provide a celebration ceremony similar to the one in Step 3 of Skill #1.

I can pretend with my friends by:	
Talking like my character	Yes Maybe? No
Looking like my character	Yes Maybe? No
Acting with my body like my character	Yes Maybe? No
Saying and doing what I need to do when it is my turn	Yes Maybe? No

Figure 66. Self-management chart for pretending with others.

STEP 4

Use—Earning the Fourth Puzzle Piece

Framework Step	The Teacher Will:	The Children Will:
Step 4 **USE**	Teach the children to use the skill in natural settings.	Use the skill with others in a school or home setting.

Create opportunities to practice this skill in the natural environment by scheduling a center time activity with materials and costumes centered around the interests of the children (e.g., firefighter costumes and props, magician costume and props). Prime children before center time, reminding them that "this might be a good time to do some pretending while you're playing with your friends." Before center time begins, review a chart such as the one in Figure 66 with each child. Meet with children afterwards and let them use the chart to evaluate themselves.

Use token reinforcement by using the Oscar chart from Step 2 to record naturally occurring instances of pretend play. Provide social praise and primary reinforcers when you catch children pretending.

Challenge for Step 4. Remind students that they have been practicing using roles to pretend with their friends. Then, challenge them to create a new skit with their friends. Tell them,

Make up or pick a story that you would like to act out with your friends. At the end of the week, we will see how you have developed your skit by having you perform for us. I will be looking for you to pretend to be, talk like, or act like another person or thing. Or you can pretend with your dolls or action figures. We will use our charts to score your performance. Work hard to get five yes answers. Then, you will have met your challenge!

Make and modify multiple copies of the chart in Figure 66 for the audience members to use to evaluate each skit participant. When each child has met the challenge, provide a celebration ceremony similar to that in Step 4 of Skill #1.

STEP 5
Explain—Earning the Fifth Puzzle Piece

Framework Step	The Teacher Will:	The Children Will:
Step 5 **EXPLAIN**	Teach the children the rationale for using the skill.	Say why the skill is effective in interacting with others.

In this discussion, use the principles of Social Thinking® to help the children explain why this is an important skill. Start by discussing the following with children: "Friends, we have had lots of fun becoming other things or people for just a short time. We have been practicing pretending with others. Can anyone tell me why this might be important?" Shape answers such as:

- It helps me understand what other people might do or say.
- It makes me think about how other people might feel or think by pretending.
- I have learned how to talk and interact with friends better by watching and performing with them.

Assign each child a peer buddy and ask the pair to make a list of reasons why it is important to pretend with others. After each pair has completed the list, assist the children in combining the lists to create a group poster.

Challenge for Step 5. Set up a new challenge by selecting a story the students know well and can act out as a group. Help the students to assign roles and gather props. For example, you might have the group act out their version of *The Wizard of Oz*. Make this task exciting and open-ended to students' creative interpretations. Have students complete the self-management chart in Figure 67 each day after play practice. At the end of the week, look at the charts with the students, then ask them why each social skill is important. Once students can answer appropriately, they have met the challenge. When each child has met the challenge, provide a celebration ceremony similar to the one in Step 5 of Skill #1.

While Pretending With Others . . .			
Did I learn something new about how other people think?	Yes	Maybe	No
Did I learn something new about how other people feel?	Yes	Maybe	No
Did I learn something new about why people do things?	Yes	Maybe	No
Overall, I learned about how to interact better by performing with friends.	Yes	Maybe	No

Figure 67. Self-management chart for group play.

You can expand on this celebration by having the students put on their play for another class or group of teachers or parents.

STEP 6
Adjust—Earning the Sixth Puzzle Piece

Framework Step	The Teacher Will:	The Children Will:
Step 6 ADJUST	Teach the children to use flexible thinking and problem solving.	List and demonstrate an alternative action whenever the social skill is not effective.

Start a discussion by saying: "We've been pretending with others and talking about why it's important. Now we are going to think about whether or not it's a good time to pretend." Follow up by asking children to consider this scenario: "What happens if you are in class and a friend asks you to pretend to be a car with a loud motor, and the teacher is talking?" Shape answers such as:

- Well, I might get in trouble.
- The teacher would not like it.
- The other kids would wonder why I did it.

Reinforce their answers by saying,

I agree! There are times that it is not a good time to pretend. Others might wonder why you were pretending. They might even think that you are strange because it was not the right time or place. And, if an adult is around, you will probably get in trouble.

Continue with the scenarios until the children are able to answer fluently. Develop a cue card with the children that summarizes when it's okay and when it's not okay to pretend. Some times that it might be okay to pretend include recess, lunch, and home. Times that students may find that it's not okay to pretend include reading, math, and P.E..

Continue the discussion with a new scenario: "What happens if you are playing Superman with a friend, and your friend wants both of you to fly off the top of a tall and long staircase?" Shape answers such as:

- I might get really hurt if I do.
- I probably will get in trouble.
- I might break something.
- I could hurt my friend.

Reinforce their thinking by saying, "Right on, friends! There are times that it might be unsafe or dangerous to pretend. You could hurt yourself or someone else, and you might break something that is not yours." Continue with similar scenarios until all children are able to answer quickly. Help the children describe safe ways to pretend and unsafe ways to pretend during the appropriate times they listed on their cue cards (e.g., recess).

Use cognitive behavioral interventions to help the children think through the consequences of pretending. Set up this situation:

So, friends, consider this: You are in P.E. class, and the teacher is talking. Your friend asks you to pretend that you are Batman, and he is Robin. You talk about getting on top of the bleachers and hiding from the villains. You even talk about jumping off the side of the bleachers to get away from the villains. You may even get excited about playing. Meanwhile, the teacher finishes explaining to the class about the game of dodgeball. The class is about to start playing dodgeball. Should you pretend with your friend? Let's think about this and make a picture that represents what might happen in this situation

Help the students create consequence maps of what might happen in this situation. Review the maps so the children have multiple examples of the consequences of their choices. Then, start a discussion that helps children plan out good times to use the skill of pretending:

Okay friends, it is time to make plans about pretending. So when a friend wants you to pretend with him, stop and ask yourself these questions:

o   Is it the right time?
o   Is it okay to pretend and play this game?
o   Is it the right place?
o   Is it safe to pretend and do what I am thinking?

Think about and decide what to do:
o   If it's the right time and safe, then go ahead and do it!
o   If it is not the right time and/or not safe, then stop and don't do it.

Friends, I think you are terrific! You have learned about the times it is safe and appropriate to pretend and when it is not. Remember to stop and think and make your plan before you put it in place! Now, get an index card out and write or draw some reminders about your plan for pretending. You can carry it with you wherever you go.

Use principles of Discrimination Training to make sure children know the difference between what's real and what's not real and what's true and what's not true. Help the children make a list such as this one:

Real	Pretend (Not Real)
Mom and Dad	Batman and Superman
Teachers	Cartoon characters
Brothers and sisters	Characters in video games

Challenge for Step 6. Tell students,

This is it! This is the final challenge for pretending with others. I want you to pick a card out of my hat and read about a problem I've written on the card. I want you to work with a friend to determine whether or not to pretend. When you have shared your plan with me, you'll have met your challenge!

When each child has met the challenge, provide a celebration ceremony similar to that in Step 6 of Skill #1.

Note About Additional Games

If your students have mastered the 10 games presented here, you can access a free download with five additional games that covers more advanced social skills by going to http://www.prufrock.com/assets/clientpages/pdfs/social_skills_bonus_games.pdf.

CHAPTER 7

Adapting the Puzzle Framework for Early Learners

There are several important prerequisites that are necessary for success in using the Complete the Puzzle framework. In some cases, these skills will need to be taught with intensive ABA instruction. We suggest specifically teaching the skills of

- *attending*: teach the children to attend to people, things, and activities; attend to what others are attending to; and shift their attention from thing to thing;
- *waiting*: teach the children to wait for things and attention;
- *following directions*: teach the children to follow single step directions, multiple step directions, and directions given to groups; and
- *taking turns*: teach the children to take turns with an adult, one other child, and several other children.

My Turn, Your Turn

One game that can be used to teach prerequisite skills is called My Turn, Your Turn. Find an activity that is interesting and motivating to the child. In the beginning, it might be best to start with a toy that runs down after a short period of time. For example, a See 'n Say® toy is ideal. Say "your turn" and let the child pull the string and listen to the toy. Then, say "my turn" and pull the string yourself. Alternate several short turns until the child begins reaching for the toy when you say, "your turn." The next time the child reaches, hold the toy just out of the child's reach and look expectantly for the child to make a sound or look up at you, or even better, say "my turn." If the child is highly motivated, continue to press for the child's verbal request for a turn. Use shaping to reward successive approximations of a request for a turn. Provide many sessions and be sure to end each session just before the child tires of the activity. Use lots of different toys, always beginning with keeping your own turn very short and letting the child's turn be long enough that the child enjoys the toy. Gradually even out the amount of time with the toy. You might even try food items (taking turns taking one item from the bowl). In this case, however, make sure the child finishes eating before you take your turn and that you require the child to wait for you to finish before taking another turn. Otherwise, it can become one continuous eating session.

Remember to:

- Choose highly motivating activities.
- Keep your language simple and focused on "my turn, your turn."
- Keep the periods short.
- Gradually increase the length of your own turn.
- Use a wait card or picture if necessary (see Figure 68).
- Use "my turn, your turn" cue cards if necessary.
- Allow time for the child to process what is said and done.

ADAPTING GAMES FOR EARLY LEARNERS

On the next few pages, we have provided a sample game that is adapted for early learners. We believe that many of the games in the book can be adapted in a similar manner. The major difference is a four-piece puzzle framework (see Figure 69). The steps of Talk and Explain have been eliminated. These two steps require advanced language skills that early learners have not developed. The steps recommended for early learners include Play, Act, Use, and Adjust. With early learners, you may or may not want to give them a challenge to have them earn the puzzle pieces. In some cases, just working through the steps may be enough to give the students a puzzle piece. In our sample game, we've provided challenges for the last two steps only.

Figure 68. Wait card for helping early learners.

Bingo: Getting the Attention of Another Person

STEP 1

Play—Earning the First Puzzle Piece With Bingo

Use an adapted game of Bingo to teach the skill of getting another person's attention. Use Bingo cards with highly interesting pictures. To set up the game:

1. Give each child a Bingo card.
2. Appoint one person to pull out Bingo balls/pictures (caller).
3. Appoint another person to hold the chips (poker chips or tokens of any sort that can be used to mark a picture that has been called).

Directions for play. To play the game:

1. The caller pulls out a picture, holds it up, and names it.
2. Players who have the matching piece raise their hands and say, "I need a chip!"
3. Steps 1 and 2 are repeated until at least one board is covered with chips.
4. When all pictures are covered, the winner yells "Bingo!"

Teaching the game. Explain to the students: "You are the players. Your goal is to listen to the caller and look at the picture the caller shows you. Watch this." Demonstrate the Bingo process to the children. The caller picks out one picture,

The Complete the Puzzle Framework for Early Learners

The Complete the Puzzle Framework Steps		The Teacher Will:	The Children Will:
Step 1 **PLAY**		Teach the children to play the game that requires the use of the targeted social skill.	Use the targeted social skill in a fun and engaging game.
Step 2 **ACT**		Teach the children to demonstrate the skill in a contrived situation.	Act out the skill in a role-playing or engineered situation.
Step 3 **USE**		Teach the children to use the skill in natural settings.	Use the skill with others in a school or home setting.
Step 4 **ADJUST**		Teach the children to use flexible thinking and problem solving.	Persist with the skill and/or demonstrate an alternative action whenever the social skill is not effective.

Figure 69. The Complete the Puzzle Framework for early learners

holds it up, and names the picture. Ask the children to check carefully to see if there is a corresponding picture on their card. If so, hand each child a chip to place on top of the picture. Repeat this several times until the children start pointing to the pictures, reaching for the chips, or exclaiming, "I've got that!"

Now tell children, "Let's practice asking for the chip. You can say, 'I need a chip, please!' or 'Please give me a chip!'" Demonstrate the next step: the chip holder holds up chips and gives a chip to each child who asks for one. If necessary, give the chip first, followed by a pretzel or small candy.

Practice a few rounds individually and then start the game. Remind the children of the rules: "Look at the caller's picture. If you have the picture, raise your hand, look at the chip holder, and say, 'I need a chip, please!'"

Play the game many times, giving the children plenty of practice asking for the chips. When possible, have the children vary the words and intonation of their requests, such as:

- "Can I have a chip, please?"
- "May I please have a chip?"
- "I need a chip, please."
- "Can I have one?"

Once the children are comfortable playing the game, increase the effort it takes them to get the caller's attention. Prompt them to use the caller's name, orient toward or look at the caller, tap the caller on the arm, or raise their voices. If necessary, prompt them to walk around in front of the caller.

STEP 2
Act—Earning the Second Puzzle Piece

Tell the children,

We're going to practice the skill of getting someone's attention. We practiced in the Bingo game and we talked about it. Now, we'll get to learn more about effective ways of getting someone's attention. When you use a skill effectively, it works and you don't make anyone mad. So let's see if you can tell which ways to get attention are effective. If it's effective, give a "thumbs up." If it's not effective, give a "thumbs down."

Once children understand the instructions, perform actions of getting attention that are both effective and ineffective such as:

- Yell out to a colleague, "Hey you, look over here!" (Thumbs down)
- Ask a colleague politely and quietly, "Hey, Miss Anne, look at this!" (Thumbs up)

Use additional demonstrations as needed to get accurate responses. Then say something like, "Let's look at what makes those effective." Show a voice volume

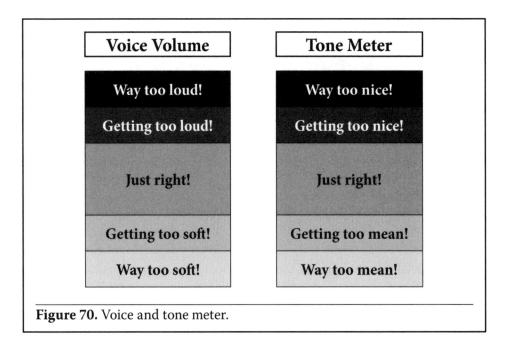

Figure 70. Voice and tone meter.

and/or voice tone indicator such as the ones in Figure 70. Practice the right tone and volume.

Then, set up role-playing situations for further practice:

Actor 1: *Mom is reading a book.*
Actor 2: Hey, Mom, look at my homework!

Actor 1: *Group is working on a mural.*
Actor 2: Look, Emma—I drew a butterfly.

STEP 3

Use—Earning the Third Puzzle Piece

Step 3 asks that students learn to use the skill in their natural environment. Provide multiple opportunities for the students to try to get your attention. For example, you could assign a project and not give the students all of the materials they need. To increase the chance the children will use the skill on their own, try out some of these strategies:
- Keep visual supports around the room to remind children to use the social skill.
- Review pictures of the role-plays or watch videos of the social skill in action.

- Post a token economy for each child in a place that's easy to see.
- Keep the puzzle framework in clear view.
- Use a self-management chart to help each child monitor his or her own progress.

Challenge for Step 3. To challenge students during this step, let them know that you'll be watching them to see that they know how to get someone's attention. Use a token economy that seems appropriate and motivating for your children to keep track of how many polite requests for attention the students make. When they each have made 10 polite requests, they earn puzzle piece #3. When all of the students have met the challenge, celebrate!

STEP 4
Adjust—Earning the Fourth Puzzle Piece

Ask children, "What are some good things to do to get someone's attention?" If necessary, prompt answers such as:
- Call a person by name in a "just right" volume and a "just right "tone.
- Say it again.
- Wave our arms (just a little bit).
- Say it louder (only a little louder).
- Touch a person on the arm (but not too hard).

Challenge for Step 4. Remind students of what they've been learning before sharing a challenge with them:

So, we've been working on a social skill called "getting someone's attention." We learned to call the person by name or tap the person gently on the arm. Then, we learned to use the right volume (not too loud nor too soft) and the right tone of voice (quiet, questioning, polite tone, not too nice or sing-song, not too mean). To earn your puzzle piece for Step 4, it's your challenge to come up with ideas for how to get someone's attention when what we've learned so far is not working.

If necessary, prompt answers such as "Say please" or "Call the person by name." Once students are able to show you how they can get attention in different ways, celebrate their accomplishments by giving them their puzzle pieces and reinforcers. You can look at the celebration for Step 6 of Skill #1 in the previous chapter for ideas.

Strategies for Teaching Early Learners

ERRORLESS LEARNING

Errorless learning was introduced by Terrace (1963) and is a procedure that maximizes the possibility of a correct response by beginning instruction with full prompting. For example, when teaching a child the answer to a question such as "What is this?" the teacher should immediately say "Train." It could also mean eliminating the opportunity for incorrect choice selection. For example, when teaching a child to point to a picture of an apple, first put out only the apple picture, or put out a picture of an apple and a blank card. Last, it might mean physically prompting a child to put toys in a basket while saying, "Let's clean up the toys."

Errorless learning uses most-to-least prompting. The teacher provides whatever prompt is needed to ensure a correct response and fades the prompt gradually so that children do not have the opportunity to make mistakes, develop bad habits, or learn incorrectly. The value in using errorless learning procedures is that it reduces frustration and the probability of future errors. In addition, it increases the time for instruction and decreases the time that might otherwise be spent reteaching things that were learned incorrectly.

PICTURE EXCHANGE COMMUNICATION SYSTEM (PECS)

Lori Frost and Andy Bondy developed The *Picture Exchange Communication System* (PECS) in 1985 (see Frost & Bondy, 2002) to teach children with autism pivotal communication and social skills. The system is based on the broad principles of ABA using what is motivating and reinforcing to children to elicit spontaneous communication through a picture exchange. During early exchanges, the children learn the power of communication, as once the picture exchange occurs, then the child is delivered what is reinforcing to her.

After the initial phase is mastered, the following phase in instruction focuses on generalizing the exchange by adding distance and sabotaging the exchange to promote persistence in the child. The next stages work on broadening language to include discriminating pictures, commenting, creating descriptive sentences, and requesting help and/or a break.

SIGN LANGUAGE

Sundberg and Partington (1998) cited research showing sign language to be an effective mode of communication for nonverbal children. As with any alternative mode to oral language, sign language has both advantages and disadvantages. According to Sundberg and Partington (1998), the advantages might outweigh the disadvantages for some children.

For children with autism who often may not imitate verbal responses effectively, teaching the spoken word can be challenging. It is much easier to prompt a child to form a sign with his hands, and when teaching the sign, the sign itself proves to be a visual prompt for the child as the symbol made is a close replication of what the object actually looks like. Furthermore, when teaching the signs, it is often easier to fade a physical prompt.

When paired with the spoken word, the use of sign language could later lead to spontaneous verbal speech. Teaching children to use sign language gives them an outlet to communicate to others what they want and need, creating children who are less frustrated and better understood.

VERBAL BEHAVIOR

The Verbal Behavior (VB) or Applied Verbal Behavior (AVB) approach is a highly prescriptive teaching process that includes the use of principles of ABA strategies to teach language skills. Motivation is key to the AVB approach; thus, it often begins with teaching mands (requests) as they often result in direct, natural reinforcement. Tacts (or labels) are taught early as well, often through pairing echoic (vocal imitation) responses with the objects they represent. Intraverbals are verbal exchanges. They can be responses to statements or questions or can be presented as partial or fill-in-the-blank sentences. They are introduced once a child has a repertoire of mands and tacts. Pictures or other visual supports are often used to help teach intraverbals, but these should be faded because intraverbals are considered mastered only when they are verbal responses to verbal (not visual) stimuli. Intraverbals are often used to expand language by teaching functions, features, and classes (i.e., identifying items when presented with descriptions of their use, appearance, or category).

The focus of the AVB approach is to develop verbal skills; however, for children who do not have vocal imitation skills, sign language is often used as a bridge to shape verbal language (Sundberg & Partington, 1998).

The initial steps for teaching mands with the AVB approach include:

- Pair yourself with highly preferred, highly reinforcing materials. That is, provide access to toys, videos, food, and drink, associating yourself clearly with these items.
- When a child shows interest in a particular item, provide a model of the mand (request). For example, if the child wants to go out, block the

door as the child approaches and say "Out!" If the child imitates, immediately open the door to let the child out. If the child does not echo, try again once or twice, but be sure to let the child out before any whining or crying begins.

- Use shaping to gradually increase the intelligibility and strength of the mands.
- Throughout the day, for several weeks, continue to pair yourself with highly reinforcing material, gradually introducing opportunities to echo, mand, or tact. Provide high levels of reinforcement for correct responses.

Vary the opportunities to echo, mand, and tact with easy-to-follow directions with fun toys and with motor imitation with fun objects (e.g., beating a drum, ringing bells, pushing buttons on toys that make sounds).

Conclusion

The children we know who happen to have ASD are wonderful, unique, and fascinating individuals. Although many of these children have challenges with social skills and struggle to build friendships, we know they can develop meaningful relationships with people who care about them. Sometimes, the relationships grow because the people who care tolerate or accommodate the unsocial characteristics of the children with ASD. The resulting relationships are often different from the more mutual friendships that typical children have with each other.

In this book, we shared some ideas for using games and activities for teaching key social skills. We think that when children learn skills such as making polite requests, sharing with others, conversing with others, and pretending with others, their relationships will develop with fewer accommodations and adaptations.

We recognize that children with ASD will probably always maintain their own distinctive ways of interaction, and, when needed, we do advocate being tolerant and providing adjusted expectations for them. We certainly have to find a balance between aiming to change behavior and celebrating their unique and diverse individualities. However, it is often easier to tolerate or accommodate than it is to teach and we would like to shift this balance to a strong emphasis on teaching. Of course, we believe this teaching should be through fun and engaging games and activities, and by patiently shaping the skills that will help children build the more mutual friendships that make life rich and enjoyable.

References

Alberto, P. A., & Troutman, A. C. (2013). *Applied behavior analysis for teachers* (9th ed.). Upper Saddle River, NJ: Merrill/Prentice Hall.

American Psychiatric Association. (2000). *Diagnostic and statistical manual of mental disorders* (4th ed., text rev.). Washington, DC: Author.

Ashcroft, W., Argiro, S., & Keohane, J. (2010). *Success strategies for teaching kids with autism.* Waco, TX: Prufrock Press.

Baer, D. M., Wolf, M. M., & Risley, T. R. (1968). Some current dimensions of applied behavior analysis. *Journal of Applied Behavior Analysis, 1,* 91–97.

Baker, J. E. (2003). *Social skills training: For children and adolescents with Asperger Syndrome and social-communication problems.* Shawnee Mission, KS: Autism Asperger Publishing Company.

Bandura, A. (1977). *Social learning theory.* New York, NY: General Learning Press.

Baranek, G. (2002). Efficacy of sensory and motor interventions for children with autism. *Journal of Autism and Developmental Disorders, 32,* 397–422.

Baron-Cohen, S. (1989). The autistic child's theory of mind: A case of specific developmental delay. *Journal of Child Psychology and Psychiatry, 30,* 285–297.

Bellini, S. (2006). *Building social relationships: A systematic approach to teaching social interaction skills to children and adolescents with autism spectrum disorders and other social difficulties.* Shawnee Mission, KS: Autism Asperger Publishing Company.

Bock, M. A. (2001). SODA strategy: Enhancing the social interaction skills of youngsters with Asperger syndrome. *Intervention in School and Clinic, 36,* 272–278.

Bricker, D., & Cripe, J. (1992). *An activity-based approach to early intervention.* Baltimore, MD: Brookes.

Buggey, T. (2005). Video self-modeling applications with children with autism spectrum disorder in a small private school. *Focus on Autism and Other Developmental Disabilities, 20,* 52–63.

Burke, J. C., & Cerniglia, L. (1990). Stimulus complexity and autistic children's responsivity: Assessing and training a pivotal behavior. *Journal of Autism and Other Developmental Disorders, 20,* 223–253.

Buron, K. D., & Curtis, M. (2008). *The 5-point scale and anxiety poster.* Shawnee Mission, KS: Autism Asperger Publishing Company.

Carr, E. G., & Durand, V. M. (1985). Reducing problem behavior through functional communication training. *Journal of Applied Behavior Analysis, 25,* 777–794.

Carter, C. M. (2001). Using choice with game play to increase language skills and interactive behaviors in children with autism. *Journal of Positive Behavior Interventions, 3,* 131–151.

Cavagnaro, A. T. (2007). *Autistic spectrum disorders: Changes in the California caseload, An update: June 1987–June 2007.* Sacramento: California Health and Human Services Agency.

Centers for Disease Control and Prevention. (2012). *Prevalence of autism spectrum disorders. Autism and developmental disabilities monitoring network, 14 sites, United States, 2008.* Retrieved from http://www.cdc.gov/mmwr/preview/mmwrhtml/ss6103a1.htm

Charlop-Christy, M. H., & Daneshvar, S. (2003). Using video modeling to teach perspective taking to children with autism. *Journal of Positive Behavior Interventions, 5,* 12–21.

Cooper, T. E., Heron, T. E., & Heward, W. L. (2007). *Applied behavior analysis* (2nd ed.). Upper Saddle River, NJ: Prentice Hall/Merrill.

Elliott, S. N., Racine, C. N., & Busse, R. T. (1995). Best practices in preschool social skills training. In A. Thomas & J. Grimes (Eds.), *Best practices in school psychology-III* (pp. 1009–1020). Washington, DC: National Association of School Psychologists.

Engelmann, S. (1968). The effectiveness of direct verbal instruction on IQ performance and achievement in reading and arithmetic. In J. Hellmuth (Ed.), *Disadvantaged child* (Vol. 3, pp. 339–361). New York, NY: Bruner/Mazel.

Frost, M. S., & Bondy, A. (2002). *The Picture Exchange Communication System training manual.* Newark, DE: Pyramid Products.

Gray, C. (1995). *Social stories and comic strip conversations: Unique methods to improving social understanding.* Arlington, TX: Future Horizons.

Gray, C. (2010). *The new social story book: Revised and expanded 10th anniversary edition.* Arlington, TX: Future Horizons.

Hart, B., & Risley, T. (1975). Incidental teaching of language in the preschool. *Journal of Applied Behavior Analysis, 8,* 411–420.

Heflin, J., & Simpson, R. (1998). Interventions for children and youth with autism: Prudent choices in a world of exaggerated claims and empty promises: Part II: Legal/policy analysis and recommendations for selecting interventions and treatments. *Focus on Autism and Other Developmental Disabilities, 13,* 212–220.

Horner, R. H. (2000). Positive behavior supports. *Focus on Autism and Other Developmental Disabilities, 15,* 97–105.

Individuals with Disabilities Education Improvement Act, Pub. Law 108–446 (December 3, 2004).

Kaplan, J. S., & Carter, J. (1995). *Beyond behavior modification: A cognitive-behavioral approach to behavior management in the school.* Austin, TX: Pro-Ed.

Koegel, L. K., & Koegel, R. L. (1999). Pivotal response intervention I. Overview of the approach. *Journal of the Association for the Severely Handicapped, 24,* 174–185.

Koegel, L. K., Singh, A. K., & Koegel, R. L. (2010). Improving motivation for academics in children with autism. *Journal of Autism and other Developmental Disorders, 40,* 1057–1066.

Krantz, P. J., & McClannahan, L. E. (1998). Social interaction skills for children with autism: A script-fading procedure for beginning readers. *Journal of Applied Behavior Analysis, 31,* 191–202.

Lavoie, R. D. (1994). *Learning disabilities and social skills with Richard Lavoie: Last one picked . . . First one picked on* [Video and Teacher's Guide]. Available from http://www.ricklavoie.com/videos.html

Lovaas, O. I. (1987). Behavioral treatment and normal educational and intellectual functioning in young autistic children. *Journal of Consulting and Clinical Psychology, 55,* 3–9.

Mayer, R., Sulzer-Azaroff, B., & Wallace, M. (2012). *Behavior analysis for lasting change* (2nd ed.). Cornwall-on-Hudson, NY: Sloan Publishing.

McClannahan, L. E., & Krantz, P. J. (1999). *Activity schedules for children with autism: A guide for parents and professionals.* Bethesda, MD: Woodbine House.

McEachin, J. J., Smith, T., & Lovaas, O. I. (1993). Long-term outcome for children with autism who received early intensive behavioral treatment. *American Journal on Mental Retardation, 97,* 359–372.

McGee, G., Daly, T., & Jacobs, H. (1994). The Walden preschool. In S. L. Harris & J. S. Handleman (Eds.), *Preschool education programs for children with autism* (pp. 127–162). Austin, TX: PRO-ED.

Miller, L. J., Schoen, S., Coll, J., Brett-Green, B., & Reale, M. (2005). *Final report: Quantitative psychophysiologic evaluation of sensory processing in children with autistic spectrum disorders.* Los Angeles, CA: Cure Autism Now.

National Research Council. (2001). *Educating children with autism.* Washington, DC: National Academy Press.

New York State Department of Health, Early Intervention Program. (1999). *Clinical practice guideline: Report of the recommendations. Autism/pervasive developmental disorders, assessment and intervention for young children (Age 0–3 years).* NYSDH Publication No. 4215. Albany, NY: Author.

Noonan, M. J., & McCormick, L. (1993). *Early intervention in natural environments: Methods and procedures.* Belmont, CA: Brooks/Cole.

O'Neill, R. E., Horner, R. H., Albin, R. W., Sprague, J. R., Storey, K., & Newton, J. S. (1997). *Functional assessment and program development for problem behavior: A practical handbook* (2nd ed.). Pacific Grove, CA: Brooks/Cole.

Partington, J. W. (2006a). *The assessment of basic language and learning skills—revised.* Pleasant Hill, CA: Behavior Analysts.

Partington, J. W. (2006b). *The assessment of basic language and learning skills: An assessment, curriculum guide, and tracking system for children with autism or other developmental disabilities.* Danville, CA: Behavior Analysts.

Quinn, C., Swaggart, B. L., & Myles, B. S. (1994). Implementing cognitive behavior management programs for persons with autism. *Focus on Autistic Behavior, 9*(4), 1–13.

Saunders, A. F., & Lo, Y. (2011). *The "how to" of video modeling: Implementing the evidence-based practice.* Presented at the annual meeting of the Council for Exceptional Children, National Harbor, MD.

Schopler, E., Mesibov, G. B., & Hearsey, K. (1995). Structured teaching in the TEACCH system. In E. Schopler & G. B. Mesibov (Eds.), *Learning and cognition in autism* (pp. 243–267). New York, NY: Kluwer Academic/Plenum.

Schrandt, J. A., Townsend, D. B., & Poulson, C. L. (2009). Teaching empathy skills to children with autism. *Journal of Applied Behavior Analysis, 42,* 17–32.

Schreibman, L. (2005). *The science and fiction of autism.* Cambridge, MA: Harvard University Press.

Smith, T. (2001). Discrete trial training in the treatment of autism. *Focus on Autism and Other Developmental Disabilities, 16,* 86–92.

Snyder-McLean, L., Solomonson, B., McLean, J., & Sack, S. (1984). Structuring joint action routines: A strategy for facilitating communication and language development in the classroom. *Seminars in Speech and Language, 5,* 213–228.

Sundberg, M. L. (2008). *Verbal behavior milestones assessment and placement program: The VB-MAPP.* Concord, CA: AVB Press.

Sundberg, M. L., & Partington, J. W. (1998). *Teaching language to children with autism or other developmental disabilities.* Pleasant Hill, CA: Behavior Analysts.

Terrace, H. S. (1963). Discrimination learning with and without "error." *Journal of the Experimental Analysis of Behavior, 6,* 1–27.

Wetherby, A., & Prizant, B. (1989). The expression of communicative intent: Assessment issues. *Seminars in Speech and Language, 10,* 77–91

Winner, M. (2008). *Think social: A social thinking curriculum for school-age children.* San Jose, CA: Think Social.

Winner, M. G. (2002). *Thinking about you, thinking about me.* San Jose, CA: Think Social.

Winner, M., & Crooke, P. (2009). *Socially Curious and Curiously Social.* San Jose, CA: Think Social.

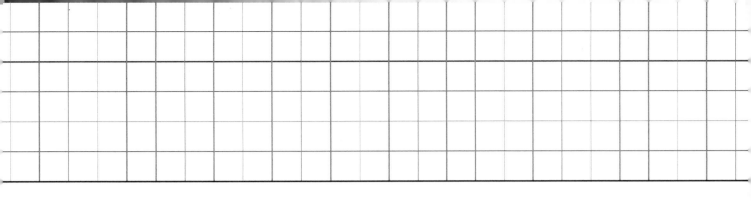

About the Authors

Wendy Ashcroft, Ed.D., **Angela M. Delloso, M.S.**, and **Anne Marie K. Quinn, M.S.**, are experienced teachers and consultants dedicated to teaching children with autism. They are known at local, state, and international levels for their evidence-based professional development and collaborative parent training sessions.